Preaching for the Planet

Sermons on Creation and Climate

— JENNY WILSON —

Sacristy Press

Sacristy Press
PO Box 612, Durham, DH1 9HT

www.sacristy.co.uk

First published in 2024 by Sacristy Press, Durham

Sacristy Limited, registered in England & Wales, number 7565667

British Library Cataloguing-in-Publication Data
A catalogue record for the book is available from the British Library

ISBN 978-1-78959-355-6

I did not say that you shall not be tempest tossed, I did not say that you shall not be work weary, I did not say that you shall not be dis-eased; but I did say, You shall not be overcome.

Julian of Norwich

Contents

Foreword

Any sermon is delivered at a particular time in a particular place to a particular audience. Sometimes the moment passes, and the text no longer connects when re-read even a few days later. Occasionally, some sermons, such as a number of these by Jenny Wilson, age like a good wine. I'm glad that Jenny has been encouraged to collect up her sermons, preached mostly at Saint Peter's Anglican Cathedral in Adelaide, so that a wider audience can taste their words, enjoy their fragrance and see their vibrant hues. Allow these sermons to swill around your mind!

Jenny reminds us to remove our layers and spend time with God. I wonder whether reading these sermons outside in nature might allow their rich wisdom to flower yet more? Nature can be a wonderful place of encounter, if we can slow down enough and notice its wonder as Jesus did. The Gospel writers record how he noticed the lilies of the field, the birds of the air, the type of soil in which seed was planted, and the fruitfulness of trees. Jenny's sermons are full of things she has noticed too. Whilst not constrained to creation care, this is the big theme included in many of the sermons in this volume.

The natural world has long been important for me. From my childhood to my education as an ecologist, and now as Bishop of Norwich and Lead Bishop for the Environment in the Church of England, I have continued to delight in God's creation. In Norfolk that includes marvelling at the peregrine falcons nesting on the spire of Norwich Cathedral, following the dancing flight of swallowtail butterflies in the Norfolk Broads, hearing the plaintive mewing of the grey seals protecting their pups on the coast, tending my own honeybees, and seeing the great dawn flight of pink-footed geese from their marshland roosting grounds to feed on the inland fields.

Tragically humanity is failing in its duty as stewards of creation. Global wildlife populations have declined by 69 per cent on average in my lifetime. Approximately 1 to 2.5 per cent of birds, mammals, amphibians, reptiles and fish have already become extinct; genetic diversity has decreased; and species are seeing dramatic habitat shrinkage. Climate change, the pressure of land use, the use of chemical controls and the desire for ever more profit all amplify this further. We need to hear the cry of creation in our age, not drown it out with excuses and an arrogant pursuit of economic gain. When the pollinators die, so will we.

I believe that every creature is a sign of God's beauty, truth and goodness—a gift from God. We are dependent on the intricate web of life. We need urgently to recover that sense of nature as a gift, seeing it not as a limitless resource and something to be exploited, but, as scripture reminds us, as the Lord's. It too needs "sabbath rest".

So, take some sabbath rest outside amongst nature. Curl up with this collection of sermons and let Jenny's reflections sink deep within you. In so doing, you will take away from this work a deeper understanding of our relationship to the natural world, and how we can be better stewards of the wonderful gift that has been given to us.

This is a thoughtful and timely collection of reflections that encourages us to think deeply about our relationship with God and the natural world, and how we can encounter God throughout our lives. Thoughtful and prayerful preaching, as shown in this volume, opens doors into wider vistas of living more as God would have us do. I hope that Jenny's prophetic voice, rooted in the scriptures, can inspire us to work to protect, conserve and restore our natural world. In such a way, we can play our part in mending the world in our own particular time and place.

+Graham Norvic
Norwich, Candlemas 2024

Preface

In January 2020, Sacristy Press published a book of my sermons entitled, *Keeping Watch for Kingfishers: God Stories.* Two women from St Peter's Cathedral in Adelaide, Di Nicholls OAM and Kathy Teague, and I met to read over four years' worth of sermons preached at the cathedral. We chose our favourite sermons, grouped them and gave them titles. We were delighted when Richard Rutherford Hilton and Natalie Watson from Sacristy Press agreed to publish the collection.

In 2023, Di, Kathy and I repeated this task with a fresh collection of sermons. This time we were keen to introduce the book with a chapter reflecting on preaching, with a particular focus on preaching in this time of climate crisis. Guided by these thoughts, Di, Kathy and I gathered six chapters of sermons commencing with one devoted to Preaching for the Planet. They make up this book.

My thanks go to Richard and Natalie for believing again in a book of my sermons, to Di and Kathy for their extraordinary devotion in choosing and collating the sermons, to John Hamilton for the painting of Encounter Bay in South Australia, my "thin place", that is found on the cover of this book, and to other members of the editing team in Adelaide—Lavinia Gent and Rosie Hamilton.

My sincere thanks go also to Bishop Graham Usher, Bishop of Norwich and Lead Bishop on the Environment in the UK, for his most generous and inspiring Foreword.

Finally, I am most grateful for the support of the Dean of St Peter's Cathedral, Bishop Chris McLeod, and our fellow clergy and staff.

This book is dedicated to my family, Nicholas, Lucy and Harriet Iles, Jane, Trevor and Sara Wilson, and the people of St Peter's Cathedral for whom these sermons were preached.

Jenny Wilson
St Peter's Cathedral, Adelaide, South Australia, Lent 2024

PART 1

On preaching

On preaching

The priest, Andrew, who influenced me most as a priest and as a preacher, was not so much a great orator. That was not his style. He would stand before the congregation with a small piece of paper on which were written a number of bullet points in his easily recognizable scrawl. Andrew would usually make comments on each of the readings, though his congregation knew that his great love was the Old Testament. Somewhere towards the end of many of his sermons something strange would happen. I thought of it as the "God moment". I would find myself with tears rolling down my cheeks some days when the God moment happened. In the God moment you know that God is about, and you know God knows exactly who you are, and you know God loves you still. It was a moment of conversion.

Barbara Brown Taylor writes about the art of preaching in her book *When God is Silent*. She said of preaching:

> Sometimes I think we resemble matchmakers more than anything else. Turning one way we carry the longings of the human heart to God. Do you love us? Do you care? Turning the other way, we bring back the answer. The reason you do not know is that you have never been loved like this before. If you let me, I will dissolve your heart with love. This is the kind of dialogue that calls for economy, courtesy, and reverence in the language we use. If we speak too long, or too factually, we will never help the lovers get together. Our job is to choose the fewest best words that allow them to find one another and then to get out of the way.[1]

Andrew was a matchmaker. So is Barbara Brown Taylor.

1 Barbara Brown Taylor, *When God is Silent* (Norwich: Canterbury Press, 2013), pp. 100–1.

The thing I most remember from my study of homiletics at theological college was reading books of her sermons. She seemed skilled in the art of conversion. My memory of her sermons was that she would lead the hearer in a particular direction, giving them the sense that they knew exactly where the sermon was going to end. She would then perform some sort of "twist" that left the hearer completely disarmed. Again, I would find myself with tears rolling down my cheeks. I remember thinking to myself that I wanted to master the art of preaching in such a way that those hearing me might know that transformative knowledge—that God is about, and you know God knows exactly who you are, and you know God loves you still.

I was encouraged to contemplate the role of the priest and preacher during priestly formation when my training rector gave me a book by Eugene Peterson, an experienced pastor and writer, entitled *Under the Unpredictable Plant.* He wrote:

> What pastors do, or at least are called to do, is really quite simple. We say the word God accurately, so that congregations of Christians can stay in touch with the basic realities of their existence, so they know what is going on. We say the Name personally alongside our parishioners in the actual circumstances of their lives, so they will recognize and respond to the God who is both on our side and at our side when it doesn't seem like it and we don't feel like it. Why do we have such a difficult time keeping this focus? Why are we so easily distracted?[2]

Peterson writes passionately about the fact that here is something very important that the preacher is to do. To fail to do it is a serious neglect of the congregation's need. It matters that this word "God" is spoken. So often, though, something else happens instead. So often people are just told what to do, told how to live their lives. Peterson rages against this:

[2] Eugene Peterson, *Under the Unpredictable Plant* (Grand Rapids, MI: William B. Eerdmans Publishing Company, 1992), p. 172.

> We easily slip into the routines of merchandizing moral advice and religious comfort. Before long we find we are program directors in a flourishing business. We spend our time figuring out how to attractively display god products. We become skilled at pleasing the customers. Before we realize what has happened, the mystery and love and majesty of God, to say nothing of the tender and delicate subtleties of souls, are obliterated by the noise and frenzy of the religious marketplace.[3]

We preachers are not there simply to tell people what to do. This is frightening. So often when the preacher first reads a passage of scripture, the temptation seems to be immediately present: God or Jesus wants us to behave in this way and we should tell the congregation how to follow their advice.

When I read Walter Brueggemann's books about the use of imagination in preaching, I began to think more critically about how preaching as an event of conversion might be nurtured or hindered. I immediately resonated with his words in *Hopeful Imagination*: "People are changed not by ethical urging but by transformed imagination."[4]

The ethical urging refers to telling people what to do, to giving instruction. The word "should" seems to have a large role to play in such preaching. I agree with Brueggemann that this is unlikely to change people. Why is this so? In response to "ethical urging" people may change their *behaviour* as a result of some of these feelings inspired by such preaching—guilt or fear, for example—but have they been *changed*? The "change" about which Brueggemann writes seems to be something more fundamental than a change in behaviour. He seems to be writing about a conversion type change—a new understanding or experience of who God is and who we are as ones created by God. When I left church after an "Andrew sermon", it was not that I was sent out with a new set of things to do, a new set of behaviours. Instead, *the world looked different.*

---

3 Peterson, *Under the Unpredictable Plant*, p. 173.

4 Walter Brueggemann, *Hopeful Imagination* (Philadelphia: Fortress Press, 1986), p. 25.

Brueggemann is suggesting that this sort of change can be brought about by transforming people's imaginations.

Each of these writers, Barbara Brown Taylor, Eugene Peterson and Walter Brueggemann, seem to be pointing to a similar idea: that it is possible in a sermon to create the environment in which the hearer might be affected in such a way that they sense God's presence; that they are converted in some way; that their life is transformed in some way. Each of these writers is also pointing to another possibility—that often the hearer of the sermon is *let down* by the preacher. Brueggemann, for example, describes "ethical urging" from the preacher. Peterson, similarly, writes of the preacher "merchandizing moral advice". Barbara Brown Taylor urges the preacher to "choose the fewest best words . . . and then . . . get out of the way". The hearer of the sermon is let down by a preacher who tells them, often at length, *how to behave*.

The almost frightening challenge for the preacher is to create the environment for those who are listening to the sermon such that they might experience a *conversion-like* change. The assumption here is that there is a need for change, a need to hear this "God" word. The assumption here is that, for many or perhaps most of us, to rework the words of the mystic Julian of Norwich, "all is not well." And that, in God, with God alongside, we might glimpse the possibility that "all shall be well".

Rowan Williams on the nature of the "lovers"

Barbara Brown Taylor described preaching as "matchmaking"—our aim is to *allow [the lovers] to find one another and then to get out of the way.*[1] Two ideas from the former Archbishop of Canterbury Rowan Williams give insight into the nature of these "lovers"—human beings and God.

Rowan Williams writes with an insight into human nature and the nature of God that I have found to be at the same time disarming and profoundly helpful. One of the first books I read by Williams was *Silence and Honey Cakes*, a book which contains reflections on sayings of the desert mothers and fathers. His thoughts on the following statement left me quite shocked: "We have put aside the easy burden, which is self-accusation, and weighed ourselves down with the heavy one, self-justification."[2] Williams writes the following:

> Self-justification is the heavy burden because there is no end to carrying it; there will always be some new situation where we need to establish our position, dig the trench for the ego to defend. But how on earth can we say that self-accusation is a light burden? We have to remember the fundamental principle of letting go of our fear. Self-accusation, honesty about our failings, is a light burden because whatever we have to face in ourselves, however painful is the recognition, however hard it is at times to feel we have to start all over again, we know that the burden is already known and accepted by God's mercy. We do not have to

1 Taylor, *When God is Silent*, pp. 100–1.

2 Rowan Williams, *Silence and Honey Cakes* (Oxford: Lion Books, 2003), p. 47.

> create, sustain and save ourselves; God has done, is doing and will do all. We have only to be still . . . [3]

This illustrates how difficult it is for a human being to be open to God. We are closed in, focused on ourselves, as we attempt the endless task of asserting that we are worthwhile. The great irony is that the one who names us worthwhile, God, is waiting nearby ready to gather us into God's love. This "saying" from one of the desert fathers also has within it one mechanism by which we can be gathered into that love—"self-accusation"—which Rowan Williams describes as "honesty about our failings".

In his book *The Edge of Words*, Rowan Williams gives a description of God that resonates surprisingly closely with the description of human beings that we find in *Silence and Honey Cakes*. He writes of "the unconditional witness to which/whom [we] seek to be open"[4] and of "the 'infinite resource' of God, the reality or presence that has no interest to pursue and no selfhood to defend".[5] We have, then, a description of God as a witness whose behaviour is the opposite of our own—we are endlessly trying to justify ourselves whereas God has "no interest to pursue, no selfhood to defend". It is tempting to conclude that a witness with no defensive behaviour is utterly safe. A knowledge of C. S. Lewis' Narnia books in which God is characterized as the lion, Aslan, will quickly have one withdraw that word. The scene in which the little girl Lucy asks the beavers if Aslan is safe is unforgettable: "Safe?" said Mr Beaver, " . . . who said anything about safe? Course he isn't safe. But he's good."[6]

Discussing his own book on the Narnia books, The Lion's World, and Lent, Rowan Williams states:

---

3 Williams, *Silence and Honey Cakes*, pp. 47–8.

4 Rowan Williams, *The Edge of Words* (London: Bloomsbury, 2014), p. 89.

5 Williams, *The Edge of Words*, p. 90.

6 C. S. Lewis, *The Lion, the Witch and the Wardrobe* (London: Collins, 1998), p. 87, (Chapter 8).

> Jesus in the desert . . . looks towards God and there's nothing there that will solve a problem, nothing there that will sweep away all the questions. What there is is truth and love and patience and changeless welcome. In due course that will transform us, it will bring us to joy, it will make our problems . . . fade away. But first of all we have to get used to a new climate, we have to breathe a new air, . . . the air of the Holy Spirit . . . [we have to] get used to the idea of God quite different from what we expected and yet at the same time ringing bells with what we most care about and most deeply long for.[7]

Again, we have a description of God that gives insight into the possibility of conversion. In God's presence there is "truth and love and patience and changeless welcome". It is a presence, though, to which it may take time to become acclimatized.

It is as if a human being stands with arms tightly closed around themselves—in self-justification—whilst God stands nearby with arms outstretched. Is it possible that something enables the human being to relax their arms in a gesture of vulnerability? It is only when the human being is exposed in this way that God can embrace them. What is it that enables a human being to relax their arms? Is it possible for a preacher in their sermon to nurture the possibility of such a miracle?

As we explore ways of preaching for the planet, preaching for all things loved by God, in a time where our planet's health is in peril, when a pandemic has clutched at human capacity to thrive, when wars continue to plague the earth, how might we preach in such a way that the moment of conversion we hope to nurture in our congregations might help us in working for healing? How might we encourage when the enormity of the problem seems only to bring discouragement, even despair? How might we inspire faith that God is alongside us in creating, redeeming, and sanctifying the planet as we believe that God is alongside us in creating, redeeming, and sanctifying humanity?

---

7 #BigRead13: "Why study C.S. Lewis for Lent" with Rowan Williams *YouTube* video, 7.22. 30 January 2013. <https://www.youtube.com/watch?v=K1zBmmyVo0c>, accessed 27 February 2024.

Preaching and Exodus—"the small door through which Messiah may enter"

> The Israelites groaned under their slavery, and cried out. Out of the slavery their cry for help rose up to God. God heard their groaning, and God remembered his covenant with Abraham, Isaac, and Jacob. God looked upon the Israelites, and God took notice of them. (Exodus 2:23–4)

The story of the Exodus is told in the second book of the Bible. One of the stories that gives the deepest insight into the nature of God and the nature of humanity, the book Exodus opens with the Hebrew people in slavery under the cruel power of the Egyptian Pharoah. It is not until the final verses of the second chapter that God enters the scene, after the death of the Egyptian king. And God's entrance is in response to something. God enters the story in response to the groaning of the Hebrew people.

In his book *Interrupting Silence*, Walter Brueggemann offers this telling reflection on Exodus 2:23:

> The Hebrews are able to remember and compute the truth that they are "Israelites". . . . it is a moment . . . when the victims become conscious, when the slaves become aware that they may be actors in their own history and agents of their own future . . . The cry and the groan are the beginning of that process that eventuated in a departure from Pharoah's system. . . . they brought their suffering and pain to speech . . . in that instant they entertained, as they had not been able to before, the possibility that alternative ways of existence are available . . .
>
> Antonio Gramsci asserts that this moment is "the small door through which Messiah may enter" . . . that declaration of the unbearable was an act of hope. . . .

> Only now, only belatedly, YHWH enters the narrative. . . . For two chapters God has been noticeably non-participatory. . . . but then the silence is broken. The groan is sounded. The cry is uttered. . . . At long last God heard. . . . Their cry . . . knew where to go. The cry understood that its proper destination was the ear of YHWH, for YHWH turned out to be the listener. More than that, YHWH turned out to be the magnet that drew and continues to draw the cries and groans of the helpless, vulnerable, and indebted who move to YHWH's festival-generating mercy. As a result of the arrival of the cry at the attentiveness of YHWH, YHWH is given the full share of responsive verbs: God heard . . . God saw . . . God knew . . . God remembered . . . [and God says], "I have come down to deliver them".[1]

God enters the scene of slavery in response to the cry of the one enslaved. And then God brings freedom.

Is it possible that the preacher might enact the cry of the one enslaved?

The preacher, in a sermon, might invite the one in pain to give voice to their cry. The preacher in allowing the voice of the oppressed, the one in pain, one suffering in the early days of the Covid pandemic, a mother living in a war zone, the one around whose home seas are rising due to global warming, the planet itself, where the preacher utters their cry, their groaning in the midst of their sermon, they are again calling upon God to hear, see, know and remember. The preacher is *enacting the Exodus cry* on behalf of the oppressed, whatever their circumstances, and they call on God in the body of Christ sitting before the preacher to hear, see, know and remember, to deliver. And woven as the words of the cry are in the sermon with the words of the scriptures and the reflections of the

---

1 Walter Brueggemann, *Interrupting Silence* (London: Hodder & Stoughton, 2018), pp. 15–21.

preacher, there is hope that in the sermon there might be glimpsed "the small door through which the Messiah may enter".

The invitation of the preacher to the cry of the oppressed may occur in the preacher speaking the words of the oppressed. In a sermon about global warming, I told the story of two women whose homes were being destroyed by global warming, who read a portion of a poem they had written. In a sermon in the early days of the pandemic, on the 200th anniversary of Florence Nightingale's birth, I read from a Facebook post by Julienne, an ICU nurse in New York City. At a time when bushfires literally destroyed an Australian country town, I read from the statement of the mayor of that town.

But the expression of the cry in our sermons might not always be in words. When Russia invaded Ukraine, I described in a sermon two photographs seen in news reports: one of an old lady with outstretched arms in front of Saint Michael's Cathedral in her home city, and one from a newspaper picture which showed a row of schoolchildren sitting like parcels on supermarket shelves, their faces covered in masks, preparing for a bombing raid in Druzhkivka. In preaching for the planet, a photograph of a nearly extinct species of bird helped our reflections. A photograph expresses a cry for God to enter the scene, to see, know, remember, come down to deliver.

Preaching and the voice of the Prophets—"the power of utterance"

> Get you up to a high mountain,
>   O Zion, herald of good tidings;
> lift up your voice with strength,
>   O Jerusalem, herald of good tidings,
>   lift it up, do not fear;
> say to the cities of Judah,
>   "Here is your God!" (Isaiah 40:9)

In his book, *The Word Militant: Preaching a Decentering Word*, Walter Brueggemann reflects on the art of preaching. In the essay, "At Risk with the Text", he expresses great faith in the power of utterance.[1] He describes the voice of longing that he imagines to be present in those who are waiting for the sermon:

> Is there any word from the Lord? (Jeremiah 37:17) We reach out, in fear and hope, to be addressed by newness, because we know the human spirit will wither if there is no address.[2]

The prophet Isaiah, speaking in the context of the exile of the people of Israel in Babylon, responds: "Here is your God!" (Isaiah 40:9) [Brueggemann reflects . . .] The very utterance opened a new possibility that the poet will present ··· Brueggemann, who describes his preacher

---

1 Walter Brueggemann, *The Word Militant: Preaching a Decentering Word* (Minneapolis: Fortress Press, 2010), pp. 1–20.

2 Brueggemann, *The Word Militant*, p. 3.

as a poet, gives to that poet extraordinary creative power: The poet in vivid imagination can create:[3]

> This is indeed a word from the outside . . . a word that comes in the way of poetry, that offers no explanation, no certainty, no accommodation to the agents of surveillance. It is a moment of utterance! . . . everything has now been changed by the poetic utterance, because the poetry cannot be unsaid . . . The word has been uttered and the juices of alternative possibility have begun to flow.[4]

I found this quite staggering when I first read it. When the preacher/poet utters a word of hope, in the voice of the prophet proclaiming the presence of God, speaking comfort in the voice of God, that utterance has power. The power to give hope. And that utterance cannot be removed, cannot be unsaid. That utterance exists and so "everything has now been changed". Brueggemann is clear that this utterance gives no certainty, but the hearer surely suspects that nothing that matters gives certainty. The utterance has given hope.

The preacher may invite into their sermons the voice of the prophets, the prophets of the scriptures, certainly, but also the prophets of our time and place.

The prophet Isaiah, for example, offers not only the most profound words of comfort and identity to God's people:

> Do not fear, for I have redeemed you;
> I have called you by name, you are mine. (Isaiah 43:1)

Isaiah also speaks words of the utterly surprising creativity of God, especially in places of suffering:

---

3 Brueggemann, *The Word Militant*, p. 7.

4 Brueggemann, *The Word Militant*, p. 8.

> Do not remember the former things,
> or consider the things of old.
> I am about to do a new thing;
> now it springs forth, do you not perceive it?
> I will make a way in the wilderness
> and rivers in the desert. (Isaiah 43:18–19)

As we preach in the circumstances of our time and place, it is to our own prophets that the preacher might turn for the words of inspiration and challenge and hope. As we preach for our planet in its time of direst need, for example, our prophets are David Attenborough and Greta Thunberg, to name just two.

In two separate interviews David Attenborough said the following:

> We've seen albatrosses come back with their belly full of food for their young and nothing in it. The albatross parent has been away for three weeks gathering stuff for her young and what comes out? What does she give her chick? You think it's going to be squid, but it's plastic. The chick is going to starve and die.[5]

> Plastic manufacturers happily say when you've used it throw it away, discard it. There is no away. Plastic is so permanent, so indestructible that when you've cast it into the ocean it does not go away. . . . I am certain that when people understand the consequences of what they are doing that they will care for the rest of the world in a profound way . . . There are simple things that we can do.[6]

A preacher might put the few words, "there is no away", in a sermon and those listening will *feel* David Attenborough's longing for change, will *feel*

---

5 <https://www.theguardian.com/environment/2017/oct/15/david-attenborough-urges-immediate-action-on-plastics-blue-planet>, accessed 27 February 2024.

6 <https://www.youtube.com/watch?v=cX1T79ZKJqM&feature=youtu.be>, accessed 27 February 2024.

God's longing for change . . . We don't need to say much more . . . leave those listening with the feeling . . .

Another powerful voice for the healing of creation is that of Greta Thunberg. Addressing the European Union Council about the desperate state of our planet, she spoke of a "sixth mass extinction". As she did so, her voice faltered:

> The extinction rate is up to six times faster than what is considered normal, with up to 200 species becoming extinct every single day . . . It is still not too late to act. It will take a far-reaching vision, it will take courage, it will take fierce, fierce determination to act now, to lay the foundations where we may not know all the details about how to shape the ceiling. In other words, it will take cathedral thinking. I ask you to please wake up and make changes required possible.[7]

It is as if those such as Greta Thunberg, Tim Flannery and David Attenborough, *accompany* us in our sermons; their presence, their words, help God to bring about the conversion for which God longs.

---

7 <https://www.theguardian.com/environment/2019/apr/16/greta-thunberg-urges-eu-leaders-wake-up-climate-change-school-strike-movement>, accessed 27 February 2024.

Preaching and the writers of wisdom

> [Christ] is the image of the invisible God, the firstborn of all creation; for in him all things in heaven and on earth were created, things visible and invisible . . . all things have been created through him and for him. He himself is before all things, and in him all things hold together. . . . For in him all the fullness of God was pleased to dwell, and through him God was pleased to reconcile to himself all things, whether on earth or in heaven, by making peace through the blood of his cross. (Colossians 1:15–20)

Scripture

Sermons are often enhanced by quotations from the writers of wisdom. Certainly, the scriptures are an excellent source for such quotations! The passage from Colossians 1, known as the "Colossians Hymn", poetically expresses Christ's profound involvement in the creation and redemption of "all things". One scholar wrote that the words "all things" ring like a bell through this passage, making it very clear that God's redemption is not only for all humanity but for all creation. This is essential theology for our preaching for the planet.

Laudato Si'

Pope Francis, in his encyclical *Laudato Si'*, has an excellent chapter on the scriptural basis for care of creation. The place we must start, of course, is Genesis.

> The creation accounts in the Book of Genesis contain, in their own symbolic and narrative language, profound teachings about human existence and its historical reality. They suggest that human life is grounded in three fundamental and closely intertwined relationships: with God, with our neighbour, and with the earth itself. . . . these three vital relationships have been broken, both outwardly and within us. This rupture is sin. The harmony between the Creator, humanity and creation as a whole was disrupted by our assuming the place of God and refusing to acknowledge our creaturely limitations. This in turn distorted our mandate to "have dominion" over the earth (cf. Genesis 1:28), to "till it and keep it" (Genesis 2:15). As a result the originally harmonious relationship between human beings and nature became conflictual. (*LS* 66)
>
> [We need instead] a relationship of mutual responsibility between human beings and nature. . . . "The earth is the Lord's" [Psalm 24 says in verse 1], "to him belongs the earth with all that is within it" [we find in Deuteronomy 10:14]. (*LS* 67)[1]

Pope Francis continues reflecting on the purpose in God's eyes of each creature:

> Our insistence that each human being is an image of God should not make us overlook the fact that each creature has its own purpose. None is superfluous. The entire material world speaks of God's love, his boundless affection for us. Soil, water, mountains: everything is, as it were, a caress of God. (*LS* 84)

Pope Francis concludes his reflection on a scriptural basis for "our care of our common home", as *Laudato Si'* is subtitled, by writing of Jesus:

> With moving tenderness he would remind them that each one of them is important in God's eyes: Are not five sparrows sold for

---

1 Pope Francis, *Laudato Si'—On Care for our Common Home* (Vatican City: Our Sunday Visitor Publishing Division, 2015).

> two pennies? And not one of them is forgotten before God. . . . The Lord was able to invite others to be attentive to the beauty that there is in the world because he himself was in constant touch with nature, lending it attention full of fondness and wonder. (*LS* 96, 97)

These thoughts from Pope Francis give just a few insights into the language that the preacher can use when giving a scriptural foundation for the godly imperative to care for the earth.

The Earth Bible Project

I was fortunate in my own studies to be influenced at theological college by the writing of The Earth Bible Project—written by a group of biblical scholars, based in Adelaide. The writings of this group followed from the idea that the *Earth* is a *character* in the scriptural texts. The *Earth* has a *voice* in scripture. I used this idea in a sermon when reflecting on the issue of plastic waste via the story of Jesus healing a leper:

> Each one of us have seen pictures in social and news media of whales with their stomachs choking in plastic bags, of birds with their stomachs filled with tiny and less than tiny pieces of coloured plastic that they are enticed into believing is food. We have seen photos of seashores covered with plastic bottles. What does God see as God looks upon our planet from the sky? A white film of plastic on the shores and seas that were to be a safe home for sea life, for human life? A white film of this substance that threatens to choke us . . . A white film not unlike leprosy, perhaps, on the planet?
>
> Does the planet cry out to God . . . "If you choose, you can make me clean"?
>
> And can we doubt that Jesus gazes on the planet with pity and compassion and raging anger at what has been done to her and replies, "I do choose, be made clean."

Elizabeth Johnson's *Creation and Cross: The Mercy of God for a Planet in Peril*

Another wonderful resource for preaching for the planet is found in the final chapter of Elizabeth Johnson's recent book *Creation and Cross: The Mercy of God for a Planet in Peril*, in which the author leads the reader on a series of imaginative exercises which she calls thought experiments, thought experiments which might inspire our preaching. The way the book is presented is unique in itself. The entire book is written as a conversation between the author Elizabeth and Clara. "With a name derived from the Latin word for clear and bright, Clara is a composite of the multitude of inquiring, insightful women and men students I have had the privilege of teaching for over half a century."[2]

Clara says to Elizabeth: "I know many people who believe in God's mercy in Christ but find it difficult to connect this faith with the ecological world, despite our discussion here. You can spell out the implications of creation, cross, resurrection, and incarnation all you want, but it feels like a giant seismic shift to rearrange the faith furniture in their head to see that all creatures are embraced by God's mercy."

Elizabeth responds: "We have already discussed a major reason for this, namely, the Western philosophy that holds humans are superior to the material world which, in turn, is made for our use. The problem resides in a tyrannical anthropology. We loom so large in our own minds that we block out the others around us. . . . [Our]goal is to live in the spirit of the burning bush, to see, hear, and 'know' the world in a godly sense."[3]

The final chapter concludes with the reader reimagining the word "us" in the scriptures. (This closely connects with the key idea of the Earth Bible Project.) When in Matthew's Gospel Jesus is called "Emmanuel—God with us" who is the "us"? When in the Prologue of John's Gospel, we read "The Word became flesh and dwelt among us" again, who is the "us"? Johnson writes: "Reimagine 'us.' Try to expand the boundaries of 'us' when you think, speak, pray, teach, preach, read, or propose

---

2 Elizabeth A. Johnson, *Creation and Cross: The Mercy of God for a Planet in Peril* (New York: Orbis Books, 2018), p. xv.

3 Johnson, *Creation and the Cross*, p. 198.

actions, in order to include other creatures along with our human selves in relation to God." [4]

Listening in on Clara and Elizabeth's conversation we have begun the imaginative process that will help us begin to make what Clara called a "giant seismic shift to rearrange the faith furniture in their head to see that all creatures are embraced by God's mercy". Ideas from the conversation between Elizabeth and Clara would greatly inform any preaching for the planet.

And then there is poetry . . .

The work of conversion can be greatly nurtured by the presence in a sermon of poetry. In a sermon for Remembrance Day, I wove two poems, one by Wilfred Owen, *Anthem for Doomed Youth,* and a poem, *Resistance*, by the Poet Laureate Simon Armitage who in 2022 had crafted a poem in solidarity with the people of Ukraine.

Michael Leunig is an Australian cartoonist, writer, painter, philosopher and poet. His commentary on political, cultural and emotional life spans more than 50 years and has often explored the idea of an innocent and sacred personal world. Leunig's poems/prayers give often breathtaking insight into the beauty and frailty of humanity. In his prayer asking God for "Another way of being, another way of knowing", perhaps the most poignant line is "Nothing can be loved at speed."[5] I used this poem at the close of an Epiphany sermon.

---

4 Johnson, *Creation and Cross*, p. 216.

5 Michael Leunig, *The Prayer Tree* (Sydney: HarperCollins, 1990), pp. 32–3.

Preaching as a walk on the Emmaus Road

> They said to each other, "Were not our hearts burning within us while he was talking to us on the road, while he was opening the scriptures to us?" (Luke 24:32)

I wonder if preaching is not unlike two disciples walking along the Emmaus Road, reflecting on things that have happened, as Jesus walked beside them asking, "What things?" The preacher, nurtured, we prayerfully hope, by the Spirit of Jesus, weaves the scripture readings from the day with the stories of the community, the country and the world at that time and place. The prayer of the preacher and the community listening to them might be that through the sermon "their hearts would burn within them", as they glimpse the possibility for those listening to the sermon, for places of war and famine and fire and flood, for the planet itself, that God is about, and that God knows exactly who they are, and that God loves them still.

PART 2

Preaching for the Planet

CHAPTER 1

He was standing in the sea

He was standing in the sea. The shore of his island behind him. His lectern—the lectern on which sat the words of his speech to those gathered in Glasgow at the COP26 summit—also stood in the sea. His nation's flag was fluttering in the breeze. "Climate change and sea level rise are deadly existential threats to Tuvalu and low-lying Atoll countries," Simon Kofe, the foreign minister of Tuvalu, said. "We are sinking but so is everyone else. In Tuvalu we are living the realities of climate change and sea level rise. As you stand watching me today at COP26, we cannot listen to speeches when the sea is rising around us all the time. Climate mobility must come to the forefront, we must take bold alternative action today to secure tomorrow."[1] In a radio interview on our own Radio National Breakfast programme, though, Simon Kofe posed a question for experts in international law: "If a country is submerged, does it still have nation status?"[2]

If a country is submerged, does it still have nation status?

We are thinking about nations, well, kingdoms, today, aren't we? We might not consult the international lawyers, though. We might wonder what the scriptures say.

---

1 <https://opecfund.org/news/small-island-developing-states-when-everything-is-at-stake>, accessed 21 May 2024.

2 <https://www.abc.net.au/radionational/programs/breakfast/tuvalu-could-be-uninhabitable-in-50-years-due-to-climate-change/13626284>, accessed 27 February 2024.

> The floods have lifted up, O Lord,
> the floods have lifted up their voice:
> [the Psalmist says]
> the floods lift up their pounding.
> But mightier than the sound of many waters,
> than the mighty waters or the breakers of the sea:
> the LORD on high is mighty. (Psalm 93:4–5)

The floods have lifted up, O Lord . . . Climate change has caused the uplifting of floods in many places, caused bushfires and storms in others, but for the people of Tuvalu and the low-lying Atoll countries, and for many of the people of our own Torres Strait Islands, the water is moving in a different way. It is rising slowly, but inexorably. It is rising so determinedly that, unless the world community responds to climate change as we hope upon hope that it must, within 50 to a hundred years this question will hold the truth: "If a country is submerged, does it still have nation status?"

In this morning's psalm, Psalm 93, the floods do not have the final voice:

> But mightier than the sound of many waters,
> than the mighty waters or the breakers of the sea:
> the Lord on high is mighty.

The Lord on high is mighty. We gather this Sunday, at the close of our liturgical year, to celebrate the Feast of Christ the King and to ponder the idea of the kingdom of God. Scholars tell us that the word for kingdom in the language of the New Testament, Greek, *basileia*, is not so much about a geographical place, an island or group of islands like the nation of Tuvalu, or an area of land on a large continent with boundaries and borders, as it is about the *reign of God*, about a world where God's love, God's guiding presence, God's forgiveness, God's delight in and longing to heal all God has created is the abiding influence.

The Gospel reading we are given as our guide this Sunday is from John's Gospel, chapter 18, John's account of Jesus' trial before Pilate. We see Pilate question Jesus about his being a king and we see Jesus respond with his own questions.

Jesus says to Pilate, “My kingdom is not from this world. If my kingdom were from this world, my followers would be fighting to keep me from being handed over to the Jews. But as it is, my kingdom is not from here.” Pilate asked him, “So you are a king?” Jesus answered, “You say that I am a king. For this I was born, and for this I came into the world, to testify to the truth. Everyone who belongs to the truth listens to my voice.” (John 18:36–7).

Everyone who belongs to the truth listens to my voice.

We know well Pilate’s reply. His question, actually. “What is truth?” The abiding sign of the kingdom is the presence of truth, the hearing of, the speaking of truth. And of ones who hear Jesus’ voice. We are reminded in John’s Gospel of Jesus imaged as the Shepherd, a symbol of a king for the people of Israel. Do you remember on Good Shepherd Sunday, we heard him say of the shepherd:

> The sheep hear his voice. He calls his own sheep by name and leads them out. When he has brought out all his own, he goes ahead of them, and the sheep follow him because they know his voice. (John 10:3–4)

We hear Jesus’ voice. Those who glimpse belonging in the kingdom of God know his voice. We would each have words of Jesus, stories of Jesus in which he speaks which mean a great deal to us. It may be a healing story like the story of blind Bartimaeus that we read a few weeks ago. Jesus said to blind Bartimaeus, “What do you want me to do for you?” Searching for Bartimaeus’ truth, helping him find the desire of his heart . . . for *this* child of God, to be given his sight. It may be the wonder of his stories, his parables. Those tales that puzzle us, delight us, trouble us, tell the truth in strange ways. Stories told with the skill of the consummate teacher who only longed for us to know, to know the love and the presence of the God he knew as Father. The story of the prodigal son—reassuring us that whatever we have done and however little remorse we might feel, God is standing with open arms to gather us home. Or the story of an encounter, such as we heard one morning this week, of Jesus’ encounter with Zacchaeus, who climbed up his tree, longing to see Jesus, being told very clearly that Jesus must stay with him at his home this day. "But do you know about me?" Zacchaeus probably said. "It's OK, I know about you," the one who is all about the truth would have said, "I still want to stay at your home today." And he helped Zacchaeus to face his truth and find freedom from it, in it, through it.

It may be his words at the direst time, at his trial, at his death. Truth spoken, cried out in fact, of the fear there, the physical and emotional anguish there, of desertion even by God, it seemed at the time, there. It may be that hearing Jesus' voice there comforts and accompanies us in our trials, our most painful times, our death, even.

"My kingdom is not from this world," Jesus said to Pontius Pilate at his trial. We might wonder about the kingdom of God, about its otherworldliness, about whether it is present at all. We might look about us at all the struggles of things, climate change, human violence, the pandemic, and the not-unexpected natural worries and sickness we experience ourselves and in the ones who are close to us. We might look at these things and wonder about this kingdom. We are told by spiritual writers that it is a kingdom that is "now and not yet". That is here but not completely here. We might ask Jesus about that.

He told parables to help us glimpse the kingdom. I think my favourite is the parable of the mustard seed. The kingdom of heaven is like a mustard seed, he said. I like to imagine a patch of soil, bare, with no seeds in it. Then, to imagine a patch of soil with just one mustard seed in it and *feel* the difference. Feel the hope in it. Feel the expectation. Feel the presence of God in it. Perhaps the kingdom of God is like that.

As we face the truth of questions of our daily lives and of our very existence, we face them in the presence of the one who the psalmist calls the LORD. Our feast this day calls Christ the King. We might call him God, or even Love.

"If a country is submerged, does it still have nation status?" asked the foreign minister of Tuvalu, Simon Kofe.

If a life is submerged, will its truth still be held in love?

One thing we know. It will not take the deliberations of international lawyers to help us know this. That if our land is submerged beneath the sea, or if someone we love is submerged by the struggles of their lives, in the reign of God we will be known and loved and remembered. Yes, Mr Kofe, your nation exists in the heart of God, in the kingdom of God. We exist in God's eyes and mind and heart always. That is the truth of which Jesus spoke. That is the truth.

CHAPTER 2

Succumbing to merciless physics

The mayor of Glen Innes Severn in New South Wales, Carol Sparkes, wrote the following:

> Heeding the advice of fire controllers and decades of scientific reports, Glen Innes Severn council last month declared a climate emergency. As the New South Wales government itself has now declared, those emergency conditions extend far beyond our shire borders and touch every community across the state.
>
> Within our borders we have seen a magnificent, humane and unstinting response from the Rural Fire Service, State Emergency Service, Red Cross, Salvation Army, NSW Police, [councillors . . .] and hundreds of community volunteers who for months now have done everything from sweep gutters to pitch tents to butter bread for sandwiches.
>
> The anger is real. The anger is justified. Because this disaster was all foreseen and predicted.
>
> Throughout this time, every effort has been made to prepare and defend both private and public properties in my community of Wytaliba, NSW, which last week succumbed to merciless physics that pay no heed to opinion, nor folklore, nor politics.
>
> Members of my family are in hospital. Two community members, my neighbours for decades, are lost to us. We have lost dozens of homes beloved by hundreds of people. An entire community has been all but wiped off the map.[1]

1 <https://www.theguardian.com/commentisfree/2019/nov/11/weve-been-in-bushfire-hell-in-glen-innes-and-the-scientists-knew-it-was-

As we read the accounts of the extraordinary bravery of residents and firefighters of so many towns encircled by fire, as we imagine water hurled at fire from fire trucks, planes, garden hoses and perhaps even buckets, . . . today, this day, we in our cathedral will witness the sprinkling of just a few drops of water on a baby, Hamish's, head. This water is the water of baptism, the water that symbolizes God's embrace, God's healing, God's great love, for Hamish, his family, and God's great love for each one of those towns, homes, people, livestock, property threatened by fire. This world is a world of love and beauty but also a world of fire, flood and threat. And what is so very terrible is that human behaviour unconsciously and consciously contributes to the love, the beauty, and also to the possibility of fire, flood and threat. As Carol Sparkes put it, she and the community she loves "succumbed to merciless physics that pay no heed to opinion, nor folklore, nor politics".

Jesus knew all these things. Our Gospel reading this morning comes from Luke's Gospel, chapter 21. We are nearing the end of this liturgical year when Luke's Gospel has been our guide and so we read Jesus' strange words about the destruction of the temple. In the verses immediately preceding, we see an act of vulnerability not unlike our pouring of a few drops of water in baptism. A widow goes to the temple.

> Jesus looked up and saw rich people putting their gifts into the treasury; he also saw a poor widow put in two small copper coins. He said, "Truly I tell you, this poor widow has put in more than all of them; for all of them have contributed out of their abundance, but she out of her poverty has put in all she had to live on." (Luke 21:1–4)

Jesus sees. He always sees. Sees deeply into human love and goodness, as well as human sin and evil. This woman gives out of all she has, he says. Just like those who fought the fires with water, courage, the sweeping of gutters and the buttering of bread for sandwiches. They gave out of all they had.

The Gospel scene then sweeps wide to the temple and what lies ahead:

---

coming?CMP=Share_iOSApp_Other>, accessed 27 February 2024.

> When some were speaking about the temple, how it was adorned with beautiful stones and gifts dedicated to God, [Jesus] said, "As for these things that you see, the days will come when not one stone will be left upon another; all will be thrown down." (Luke 21:5–6)

The scenes of bushfire devastation cannot but come into our minds. Not one stone left upon another for some who have lost homes, property, livestock, their own lives. Jesus' disciples want to know when and how these things will happen. They want certainty. We understand that. We want certainty, too. Jesus sees human nature, knows it well and can see the way things will unfold. There will be false prophets, those who purport to know the ways of God, who will come in his name to lead astray those who try to love God and be true to his commandments; kingdoms will rise against kingdoms with intensifying violence; and the Church will face persecution and hatred. Jesus wants his disciples to understand what lies ahead for them, for us.

But he assures the disciples that he will be with them.

> "I will give you words and a wisdom that none of your opponents will be able to withstand or contradict. . . . they will put some of you to death. You will be hated by all because of my name. But not a hair of your head will perish. By your endurance you will gain your souls." (Luke 21:15–19)

They will put you to death but not a hair of your head will perish . . . Jesus is putting together what seem to be contradictory thoughts but he is talking about two different realms. Two different realities. The physical world and the world of God. The world where we might gain our souls.

The scholar John Shea writes the following about Jesus' words:

> Jesus, the one who has been through it before, will be with them and give them words to say. These words, just as Jesus's silence and words during his own trial, will have a wisdom so profound they will not be able to be contradicted. The passion of Jesus is not over; it continues with those who follow him. However,

> suffering is not the whole of it. Resurrection is the deeper and more abiding truth.[2]

Death, destruction, ash-covered landscape and burnt-out buildings do not have the final say in the God narrative. Resurrection is the deeper and more abiding truth.

Our Old Testament reading from Isaiah seems to point to this truth as well:

> For I am about to create new heavens
>   and a new earth;
> the former things shall not be remembered
>   or come to mind.
> But be glad and rejoice for ever
>   in what I am creating;
> They shall build houses and inhabit them;
>   they shall plant vineyards and eat their fruit.
> They shall not build and another inhabit;
>   they shall not plant and another eat;
> for like the days of a tree shall the days of my people be,
>   and my chosen shall long enjoy the work of
>   their hands. (Isaiah 65:17–18,21–2)

They shall build houses and inhabit them and fire shall not burn them away. Perhaps Isaiah would say the same on this day, this present day.

Living in this truth is not about turning our backs on the suffering caused by fire and flood. Living this truth is about dwelling deeply in it and listening for the whisper of God there. The presence of God there.

In a cathedral we ponder these things in word and music, in silence and stone. We also ponder them gazing at flowers. There is an arrangement of flowers in the Lady Chapel this week. Elspeth, who created the arrangement of flowers, wrote the following words:

---

2 John Shea, *The Relentless Widow* (Collegeville, MN: Liturgical Press, 2006), p. 316.

> My flower arrangement in the Lady Chapel this week is my attempt to represent the impact of events symbolically and visually on our fragile environment in the past week.
>
> Fires and drought have seen devastation to bushland, animals and our precious bee population.
>
> The use of grey foliage represents ash, the aftermath of fire; the purple flowers represent the liturgical colour purple for penance, melancholy and humility; and the new green foliage as hope, for regrowth and new life.

We must act, of course, offering help wherever we can; we must do what we can to have the causes of such ferocious fires, climate change, faced by our community, our nation, the world. Then, we might reflect, in front of a bowl of ash-coloured flowers perhaps, on the preciousness of life, the frailty of life, the possibility of the God who through Christ shows us that suffering is not the whole of it.

And then, we'll hold that baby, named Hamish, in our arms and sprinkle drops of water on his head and baptize him in the name of the Father and the Son and the Holy Spirit, and we will all see this sign of God's love for him, his family, our community, the whole world.

CHAPTER 3

Poetry from two indigenous women

The disciples of Jesus are not having a good day. We are often told that Mark's Gospel portrays Jesus' disciples as frequently struggling to understand what is going on. And the disciples are certainly not doing well in chapter 9 of the Gospel. Jesus has been transfigured before Peter, James and John up a mountain, and they have heard him named God's beloved Son. As they come down the mountain, they come across a crowd in which is a man whose son is possessed by a spirit that makes him unable to speak; whenever it seizes him, it dashes him down; he foams and grinds his teeth and becomes rigid. The man asks Jesus' disciples to cast it out, but they cannot do so. It is Jesus who heals the man's son, telling the disappointed disciples, "This kind of spirit can only come out through prayer" (Mark 9:29). He seems to be saying to them that they were trying to cast out a demon on their own. That they forgot to pray.

Small wonder that when, as we heard in our reading this morning, the disciples hear of someone who does not belong to their group casting out demons in Jesus' name, they are suspicious of them, probably jealous of them. John says to Jesus, "Teacher, we saw someone casting out demons in your name, and we tried to stop him, because he was not following us." But Jesus says to John, "Do not stop him; for no one who does a deed of power in my name will be able soon afterwards to speak evil of me. Whoever is not against us is for us" (Mark 9:38–40).

We often find ourselves wondering, like Jesus' disciples, how to pray for healing or peace. How do we pray for the situation in Afghanistan? How do we pray for healing across the world in a time of pandemic? How do we pray for healing for our planet? Jesus' priority is the kingdom. Charles Elliot, who a number of years ago wrote a book entitled *Praying the Kingdom: Towards a Political Spirituality*, suggests a most helpful idea.[1] An approach to prayer that we know we cannot embark on alone. An approach that needs people of different denominations and creeds and different faiths, and perhaps people of no faith, praying together, caring together. Charles Elliot suggests that when we are praying for a situation, we remember the voice, the story, of one person in that situation. Have we heard on the news an interview with a family with loved ones in Kabul? Have we heard the story of a person whose relative has died of Covid? Have we heard the voice of those affected by climate change?

As the Season of Creation draws to a close this year, let us hear this morning the story of two women whose voices cry out for the healing of our planet:

> High up on a melting Greenland glacier, at the end of a summer three years ago from climate hell, two young women shout a poem above the roar of the wind. Aka Niviana grew up on the northern coast of Greenland; as its ice inexorably thaws, her traditional way of life disappears. And the water that melts off that ice sheet is drowning the home of Kathy Jetnil-Kijiner and everyone else in her home nation, the Marshall Islands of the Pacific. One poet watches her heritage turn to water; the other watches that same water sweep up the beaches of her country and into the houses of her friends. The destruction of one's homeland is the inevitable destruction of the other's.[2]

These women write a poem together, meeting on their two lands. Hearing their voices might be our prayer. A little of their poem goes like this:

---

1 Charles Elliot, *Praying the Kingdom: Towards a Political Spirituality* (London: Darton, Longman & Todd, 1985).

2 <https://www.theguardian.com/environment/2018/sep/12/high-ice-hard-truth-a-poetry-expedition-to-greenlands-melting-glaciers-bill-mckibben>, accessed 27 February 2024.

Do we deserve the melting ice?
the hungry polar bears coming to our islands
or the colossal icebergs hitting these waters with rage
Do we deserve
their mother,
coming for our homes
for our lives?
From one island to another
I ask for solutions.
From one island to another
I ask for your problems.
Let me show you the tide
that comes for us faster
than we'd like to admit.
Let me show you
airports underwater
bulldozed reefs, blasted sands
and plans to build new atolls
forcing land
from an ancient, rising sea,
forcing us to imagine
turning ourselves to stone.
Sister of ocean and sand,
Can you see our glaciers groaning
with the weight of the world's heat?
I wait for you, here,
on the land of my ancestors' heart heavy with a thirst
for solutions
as I watch this land
change
while the World remains silent.[3]

---

3 <https://350.org/rise-from-one-island-to-another/>, accessed 27 February 2024.

Our prayer then is to hear the voices of the two women. To pray with them. To allow the vulnerability of each one of us to sit with the vulnerability of the two poets whose homelands are disappearing before their eyes. Praying the kingdom, by sitting with one story, one or two people, allowing their struggle, their suffering to be our companion for a time. Jesus, after all, healed one person at a time, didn't he?

Jesus continues, in the passage we have as our Gospel reading this morning, to speak of what gets in the way of God, to speak of sin, really:

> If any of you put a stumbling-block before one of these little ones who believe in me, it would be better for you if a great millstone were hung around your neck and you were thrown into the sea. If your hand causes you to stumble, cut it off; it is better for you to enter life maimed than to have two hands and to go to hell, to the unquenchable fire. (Mark 9:42–4)

If your hand, or your foot, or your eye . . . Jesus is obviously exaggerating, as was the custom in religious debate at the time, but what he is getting at does matter. What causes us to sin? What gets in the way of God? The context of Jesus' words on causes of sin is the disciples failing to see that others might bring in the kingdom. For us, pondering how we might pray for the people of Afghanistan, or the healing of the pandemic caused by Covid-19, or the healing of the planet, what causes us to sin? What gets in the way of our prayers?

Sin is sometimes thought of as a failure to let God be God. Perhaps we feel so overwhelmed by the situations for which we are trying to pray that we give up. Perhaps we feel guilty about our failure to care for the planet, for example. Or we decide that the problems of countries far from our shores must have nothing to do with us. Jesus longs to bring in God's kingdom which is about healing and wholeness for all, all people, all things in creation. Being children of God means that we belong to this wider family of God, this whole creation of God. How do we not give up on our prayers?

Oscar Romero, a bishop in the Catholic Church in El Salvador, spoke out against social injustice and violence amid the escalating conflict between the military government and left-wing insurgents. In 1980,

Romero was shot by an assassin while celebrating the Eucharist. The following prayer is attributed to him. Perhaps we might make it our own.

> It helps, now and then, to step back and take the long view.
> The Kingdom is not only beyond our efforts;
> it is even beyond our vision.
> We accomplish in our lifetime only a fraction of the magnificent enterprise that is God's work.
> Nothing we do is complete, which is another way of saying that the kingdom always lies beyond us.
> No statement says all that could be said. No prayer fully expresses our faith. No confession brings perfection. No pastoral visit brings wholeness. No program accomplishes the church's mission. No set of goals and objectives includes everything.
> This is what we are about.
>
> We plant the seeds that one day will grow. We water the seeds already planted, knowing that they hold future promise. We lay foundations that will need further development. We provide yeast that produces effects far beyond our capabilities.
>
> We cannot do everything and there is a sense of liberation in realizing that. This enables us to do something and to do it well. It may be incomplete, but it is a beginning, a step along the way, an opportunity for the Lord's grace to enter and do the rest. We may never see the end results, but that is the difference between the master builder and the worker.
>
> We are workers, not master builders; ministers, not messiahs. We are prophets of a future not our own.[4]

---

4 This prayer was composed by the late Bishop Ken Untener of Saginaw, drafted for a homily by Cardinal John Dearden in November 1979 for a celebration of departed priests. As a reflection on the anniversary of the martyrdom of Bishop Romero, Bishop Untener included it in a reflection book in a passage titled "The Mystery of the Romero Prayer". The mystery is that the words of the prayer are commonly attributed to Oscar Romero, but they were never spoken by him.

CHAPTER 4

God's handiwork

Today, on 4 October, as our reflections during the Season of Creation draw to a close, we find ourselves celebrating the day dedicated to remembering St Francis of Assisi. St Francis (1181–1226), known from 1979 as the patron saint of ecology, saw God at work in creation, experienced God's presence in the natural world, sensed that in that natural world God is speaking to us. His namesake Pope Francis wrote this:

> He would call creatures, no matter how small, "brother" or "sister". Such a conviction cannot be written off as naive romanticism, for it affects the choices which determine our behaviour. If we approach nature and the environment without this openness to awe and wonder, if we no longer speak the language of fraternity and beauty in our relationship with the world, our attitude will be that of masters, consumers, ruthless exploiters, unable to set limits on their immediate needs. By contrast, if we feel intimately united with all that exists, then sobriety and care will well up spontaneously. The poverty and austerity of Saint Francis were no mere veneer of asceticism, but something much more radical: a refusal to turn reality into an object simply to be used and controlled.[1]

Over the past weeks in our cathedral, we have explored our vocation to care for creation through poetry, preaching, photographs, music and liturgy. We have looked at practical things we can do. We have also pondered the idea that scripture can be viewed through the lens

1 Pope Francis, *Laudato Si'*: *On Care for our Common Home* 11.

of ecology by imagining the earth as a character in the text, as having a voice in the Bible. One way to do this would be to imagine St Francis himself reading the texts, reading this morning's readings, perhaps, with his love of creation in mind.

What would St Francis notice, for example, in the Ten Commandments that we heard as our Old Testament reading this morning, that gift from God to the Israelite people given to Moses as they journeyed through the wilderness? The Ten Commandments divide into two groups, one dealing with our relationship with God, one with our relationship with one another. I wonder what St Francis might have noticed as he pondered the first set of commandments. I wonder if he would have pointed to the commandment about the Sabbath:

> Remember the sabbath day, and keep it holy. For six days you shall labour and do all your work. But the seventh day is a sabbath to the Lord your God; you shall not do any work—you, your son or your daughter, your male or female slave, your livestock, or the alien resident in your towns. For in six days the Lord made heaven and earth, the sea, and all that is in them, but rested the seventh day; therefore the Lord blessed the sabbath day and consecrated it. (Exodus 20:8–11)

The Sabbath commandment points to the holiness of rest—rest for us and rest for the earth. It also reminds us of the seventh day of creation when God rested and God treasured, delighted in, all that God had made. The theme of this year's Season of Creation is of Jubilee. The Jubilee is to take place every 50 years and according to biblical regulations had a special impact on the ownership and management of land in Israel. According to the book of Leviticus, Hebrew slaves and prisoners would be freed, debts would be forgiven, and the mercies of God would be particularly manifest. We are invited in our time and place to a time to consider the integral relationship between rest for the Earth and ecological, economic, social and political ways of living.[2]

---

2 <https://seasonofcreation.org/about/#2020theme>, accessed 29 February 2024.

I wonder if St Francis would have found himself thinking, in the commandments that deal with our relationships with one another, about "You shall not steal" and "You shall not covet" as he read scripture with the earth he so loved in mind. Are we stealing from the resources of the earth; are we coveting in a way that causes damage? And what of the species that have become extinct? Would the grief of God at the loss of creatures God had imagined and brought to life seem almost to come under the commandment "You shall not murder"?

Let us imagine now St Francis pondering the parable that Jesus told in our reading from Matthew's Gospel (Matthew 21:33–41). When we spend time with a parable it often helps to sit with what puzzles us or annoys us. What would have caused St Francis to wonder if he took an earth perspective on the parable of the wicked tenants? The parable tells of a landowner who planted a vineyard, put a fence around it, dug a wine press in it, and built a watchtower and leased it to tenants to care for as he went away to another country. The problem came when the landowner sent slaves and then more slaves and then his own son to collect the produce. The problem came when the landowner asked for the fruits of the vineyard to be given to him. Not only did these wicked tenants not hand over the produce, but they also took the lives of those who came on the landowner's behalf.

We can only imagine St Francis watching with horror and disbelief at the tenants' utter ruthlessness and, frankly, stupidity as they try frantically to cling to power over the vineyard and the fruits of that vineyard. St Francis might well have noticed that Jesus does not finish the parable himself but draws out of those listening the parable's conclusion … "Now when the owner of the vineyard comes, what will he do to those tenants?" Jesus asks them. They said to him, "He will put those wretches to a miserable death, and lease the vineyard to other tenants who will give him the produce at the harvest time."

Would St Francis see in this morning's parable a resonance with humanity's failure to care for the earth in our time and place? Would he watch with horror and disbelief at us as we struggle so terribly to treat this need seriously? And would he ask us the question that Jesus asked those listening to him … what will happen to those who fail to care for what has been given to them by God?

Finally, as we look at those passages of scripture that have been given to us this morning, let us imagine St Francis chanting the psalm, Psalm 19, which begins:

> The heavens are telling the glory of God and the firmament proclaims his handiwork.

St Francis would have sung this with all his heart. For this was the way he saw creation. All creation tells the glory of God, all creation proclaims his handiwork.

For five Sundays now we have worshipped in a liturgy designed to open our eyes a little more to God's love for the earth. We have reflected on scripture with the earth, and the part we play in its care, in mind. We have engaged in our cathedral with churches and denominations across the world in this Season of Creation. Today, St Francis' Day, this season draws to a close and we will turn our focus to other ways in which God would have us worship, have us care.

As we walk out of our cathedral and as we leave the Season of Creation, we might remember that we walk out on the earth. We breathe the breath of life in company with the creatures of the earth. We treasure, with God who creates and loves and redeems, the earth.

CHAPTER 5

About faith

I will lift up mine eyes unto the hills
from whence cometh my help.

When I lift up my eyes to the hills, especially in this time of spring, my thoughts go to the wildflowers that will be found there. My notice was first directed to Australian wildflowers by Bishop Bruce Rosier. After his time as bishop of a country diocese, Bruce ended his full-time ministry as a parish priest. One spring Bruce led a group of parishioners from that parish on a bushwalk. He loved the wildflowers, and he knew them by their common names and their Latin names. I met, for the first time, spider orchids and donkey orchids, fringe lilies, vanilla lilies and chocolate lilies, all sorts of pea flowers, including the bright red "Running Postman", and Bruce's wife Faith's favourite flower, a beautiful blue lily known as a "Squill". There were creamy white candle flowers, that bush version of those items so essential to our liturgies, a pink grevilia, and any number of yellow flowers. For year after year, after Bruce had shared his love of these flowers so wonderfully made by God, a few of us would go on an annual pilgrimage to the bush to re-establish this friendship. Yes, when I lift up my eyes to the hills, it is wildflowers and the love of them nurtured in me by Bruce Rosier that enter my thoughts.

For those who originally spoke the deeply loved psalm that our choir sang to us tonight the hills were not such a safe place. The hills were a place through which the people of Israel journeyed, a place of difficult terrain and ominous threat. The words of this psalm were spoken as the journey was embarked upon, a journey that had no guarantees of safety. And, so, the traveller prayed:

> I will lift up mine eyes unto the hills
> from whence cometh my help.

The first verse of Psalm 121 is a question and the remaining verses of the psalm provide the answer. Our help comes from the Lord. And who is this Lord? The Lord is the one who breathed life into creation, the creator, the one who made heaven and earth. The one who can create all things can surely guard a traveller against any threat that might oppose him on his journey.

The psalm goes on to tell us what the creator is like. In verses 3 and 4, we see three characteristics of this creator. He will not suffer our foot to be moved; in other words, God will watch closely the path on which we walk. God neither slumbers nor sleeps—so God is always at watch with us. And God "keeps" us. The word "keep" is used four times in this psalm. This "keeper" God "guards, preserves, protects and keeps safe . . ." In verse 4, the question of verse 1 is fully answered.[1] It is from this God that our help comes. God who is utterly reliable.

The final four verses of Psalm 121 shed more light on the nature of the God who protects our journey through the hills. The Lord is a defence. When some form of attack comes upon us, be it physical danger, be it human violence, be it the evil referred to in verse 7, the Lord will be with us and will defend us. In fact, the Lord will keep our soul. The very being of us, the very heart of us, is kept safe and thriving by God.

Psalm 121 concludes:

> The LORD shall preserve thy going out, and thy coming in
> from this time forth for evermore.

Walter Brueggemann, whose commentary on the Psalms sheds great insight, describes the final verse as a "benediction for travel. The traveller is safe departing and arriving, and all along the way."[2]

1 Walter Brueggemann and William J. Bellinger, Jr., *Psalms* (New York: Cambridge University Press, 2014), p. 526.

2 Brueggemann and Bellinger, *Psalms*, p. 527.

Walking in the Australian hills, one might come across plants other than the wildflowers introduced to me by Bishop Bruce. Some plants, such as the eucalyptus and the banksia, have some very intriguing characteristics. Their cones or fruits are completely sealed with resin. These cones or fruits can only open to release their seeds after the heat of a fire has physically melted the resin. Other species, including a number of shrubs and annual plants, require the chemical signals from smoke and charred plant matter to break open their seeds. Some of these plants will only sprout in the presence of such chemicals and can remain buried in the soil for decades until a bushfire brings them to life.

The hills near to us are a habitat that has woven into it the reality of bushfire. Native plants have adapted to bushfires to such an extent that fire is essential for their survival. Human beings, who for the last few hundred years have lived in settled communities on land that is naturally bush, have attempted to ensure their survival by preventing fire, controlling fire. Fires, though, will not be tamed and when they do strike, the damage they cause can be catastrophic—property, livestock and human life are at serious risk in an environment where bushfire has a natural home.

Like the hills of those for whom Psalm 121 was written, our hills, too, at times are places of difficult terrain and ominous threat. Those who live in our hills know this well. Our hills, our plains, our seas, all human lives, in fact, are woven with times of safety and times of danger, be it the safety and danger inherent in the natural environment, be it the safety or danger woven into our living in physical bodies that fall prey to sickness and death, be it the safety or danger woven into our emotional lives, as members of families, communities, nations—we love and depend upon people and people let us down.

As people of faith, we look to the hills, the places of the beauty of wildflowers, the places of the threat of fire, we look to the hills and we ask, "From where does our help come?"

As people of faith . . .

The very asking of the question in this psalm sheds light on a life of faith.

For faith is about looking to the hills and wondering about the presence of the one who made us. Faith is about looking up in times of danger and concern and calling to the one who loves us. Faith is about speaking, singing, the psalms, reaffirming the character and truth of God, always with us, always watching over us, *keeping us* body and soul in God's dear love.

We know that the fire at times consumes, bush, wildlife, property, human life. We know that the spider orchid and the blue squill lily that adorn the hills will return each year. We know that human life is woven with danger and delight, struggle and blessing.

We are people of faith. So, we speak and sing the words of the psalms. That wherever we are and whatever life holds for us, God, the one who creates, redeems, sanctifies, . . . is our *keeper*. Each day, each journey, each night we will be blessed . . .

> The LORD will preserve our going out, and our coming in
> from this time forth for evermore.

CHAPTER 6

Under the wings of God

There were three birds in the photo, in the Nature Photographer of the Year exhibition in the South Australian Museum, three water birds, standing in the water at Moreton Bay in Queensland. The photographer had positioned himself in a spot in the wet sand near some mangroves, and he waited. Eventually the three Eastern Curlews came past, just before dusk, stopping for a nap. Two of the birds have their beaks snuggled into their feathers, the third gazes into the distance.

In another photo in the exhibition, a Northern Quoll is seen hiding in a granite outcrop at Mount Emerald near Mareeba in Queensland. Its beady eyes look nervously out from its hiding place. The rocks seemed to make a place of safety for the quoll. The photograph seemed to resonate with our psalm, a psalm of protection by God . . .

> You who live in the shelter of the Most High,
>   who abide in the shadow of the Almighty,
> will say to the LORD, "My refuge and my fortress;
>   my God, in whom I trust."
> For he will deliver you from the snare of the fowler
>   and from the deadly pestilence;
> he will cover you with his pinions,
>   and under his wings you will find refuge. (Psalm 91:1–4)

The Northern Quoll needs a safe place. For this quoll, and the three Eastern Curlews in the other photograph, are all listed as vulnerable on the IUCN Red List. The International Union for Conservation of Nature Red List of Threatened Species, founded in 1964, is the world's most comprehensive inventory of the global conservation status of biological species. The species in the photographs are under threat. Through human neglect.

Is this a prayer, I wonder, our gazing at the photographs of endangered species in the Nature Photographer of the Year Exhibition at the SA Museum? A group of cathedral parishioners visited the exhibition as part of our times of reflection for the Season of Creation. Is our gazing at such vulnerable beauty a prayer?

I thought it might be so, and further to that I found hope in this for the healing of creation, from the words of Gus Speth, a US scientist and environmental advisor:

> I used to think the top environmental problems were biodiversity loss, ecosystem collapse, and climate change. I thought that with 30 years of good science we could address those problems. But I was wrong. The top environmental problems are selfishness, greed and apathy . . . and to deal with those we need a spiritual and cultural transformation, and we scientists don't know how to do that.[1]

The top environmental problems are selfishness, greed and apathy . . . and to deal with those we need a spiritual and cultural transformation, and we scientists don't know how to do that.

A spiritual and cultural transformation is where we might play our part. Where the life of reflection on scripture, reflection on nature, wrestling with the words of Jesus and the words of the prophets, might lead us into the sort of transformation that might help bring healing to our planet.

Wrestling with the words of Jesus and the words of the prophets is exactly where we find ourselves when we listen to our Gospel reading from Luke 16. In this section of Luke's Gospel, we hear Jesus telling a series of parables. The three parables of the lost sheep, the lost coin, the lost or prodigal son in chapter 15, and then parables about wealth in chapter 16, the parable of the Dishonest Steward, and then this morning's

---

1 <https://earthcharter.org/podcasts/gus-speth/>, accessed 29 February 2024.

most demanding parable about the rich man and the poor man Lazarus, starving at the rich man's gate (Luke 16:19–31).

Each one of these parables is about the lostness of humanity, the longing of God that humanity is found, the rejoicing when the lost one returns, even in the case of the dishonest manager, when he is strangely praised for finding a way to be welcomed home.

The parable we heard read this morning is designed to cause us great discomfort. Jesus tells stories to reach not so much our minds as our hearts. We might reflect on how we feel when we hear such a parable, and in the case of this parable there is an array of possible responses.

Gathering as we are in this Season of Creation to ponder God's love for our planet and the acute danger in which our home finds itself, the acute danger in which *we* find ourselves, we will spend time this morning exploring insights from the parable on this situation. How do we reflect on scripture in the light of creation?

A number of biblical scholars in Adelaide have developed what is known as The Earth Bible Project. This involves reading the Bible from the perspective of the earth, viewing the earth as a subject in the biblical text, acknowledging that the earth may have a voice in the biblical text and listening for the cry of that voice, the wisdom of that voice, and listening for God's response to that voice. Perhaps we might imagine the earth in the place of Lazarus. The earth, lying outside our gate, outside the gate of so many who live on ignoring its plight, consuming too much, damaging its ecosystems, neglecting the need to change our carbon footprint on its ground. Perhaps we might imagine the earth, ignored, crying out, covered with sores, longing to be cared for, longing for healing.

The parable tells the story of dire consequences for the ones who ignore the cry of the poor, the needy . . . in our imagination today, the cry of our planet. And the parable concludes with a conversation between Abraham and the rich man who is in torment in Hades. The rich man is pleading that a warning is sent to his family that they might change their ways, that they might take heed of the cry of the poor. Abraham then speaks the words that are the crux of the parable.

> "They have Moses and the prophets; they should listen to them."
>
> The rich man in torment in Hades replies, "No, father Abraham;

> but if someone goes to them from the dead, they will repent." Abraham says to him, "If they do not listen to Moses and the prophets, neither will they be convinced even if someone rises from the dead." (Luke 16:29–31)

If they do not listen to Moses and the prophets . . . And what did the prophets say?

> Is not this the fast that I choose:
> to loose the bonds of injustice,
> to undo the thongs of the yoke,
> to let the oppressed go free,
> and to break every yoke?
> Is it not to share your bread with the hungry,
> and bring the homeless poor into your house;
> when you see the naked, to cover them,
> and not to hide yourself from your own kin? (Isaiah 58:6–7)

The *feeling* of the parable told by Jesus is deep fear at the chasm that is described between the place of torment and the place of comfort, at the fact there is a point when it is *too late* to change our ways. The feeling of the parable is profound regret at the consequence of neglecting the plight of the poor, of leaving it too late. And this Sunday, as we reflect on the scriptures in the light of the suffering of the earth, we might sense the deep fear that we, too, have left it *too late* to attend to the plight of the earth. Jesus would have us feel this fear, and, I think, as we read and hear stories of the plight of the earth, the changes in climate, the damage to ecosystems, the vulnerability of species created and loved by God, species like the Eastern Curlew and the Northern Quoll, we do feel that fear. We do wonder . . . have we left it too late?

The scriptures speak of the ways of human beings, and they also always speak of the ways of God. The parables are no different. And we might remember that chapter 16 of Luke's Gospel is preceded by chapter 15, where we find the parables of the lost. And in those parables, we see God's longing that we might be found, be brought home, and we see

God's delight and welcome when we are found, when we are brought home.

So, what does our parable today say to us, say to the earth, that character, remember, in the story of God, the earth, in our imagination through this parable today, crying out at the gate of the well-off in our world?

The parable exhorts us to listen. Listen to the voice of God. The voice of God heard through Moses and the prophets. The voice of God heard in Jesus. The voice of God crying through the pain of the earth.

The scientist we heard earlier seemed to hint at this. Remember what he said:

> The top environmental problems are selfishness, greed and apathy . . . and to deal with those we need a spiritual and cultural transformation, and we scientists don't know how to do that.

The parable exhorts us to listen to the voice of God, and in that listening to play our part in engaging in and nurturing the spiritual and cultural revolution that is needed if the planet is to find healing. If the planet is to know itself, in the words of this morning's psalm, like the Northern Quoll seen in a photograph in the SA Museum:

> Delivered from the snare of the fowler
>   and from the deadly pestilence;
> finding refuge under the wings of God.

CHAPTER 7

A caress of God

Pope Francis, in his encyclical *Laudato Si': On Care for our Common Home*, writes:

> Our insistence that each human being is an image of God should not make us overlook the fact that each creature has its own purpose. None is superfluous. The entire material world speaks of God's love, his boundless affection for us. Soil, water, mountains: everything is, as it were, a caress of God. (*LS* 84)

As we gather in our cathedral to ponder, in this Season of Creation, how we might better care for our common home, we will be inspired by the scriptures to hear and know what creation means to God. That it is not only human beings who are dearly loved by God. But, as Pope Francis beautifully says, "soil, water, mountains: everything is, as it were, a caress of God".

We will this morning explore some hints in the scriptures of God's love of the earth, before we look at reading our passage from Exodus with creation in mind.

Any search for God's view of creation must, of course, begin with Genesis. In the first creation account in the book Genesis, the words are repeated verse by verse: God said "Let there be" as God created, and then the writer comments, "And God saw that it was good." God creates earth and heaven, lands and seas, sun and moon, plants and fish and birds and animals, and human beings, and God sees that all of this is very good.

In his encyclical *Laudato Si': On the Care for Our Common Home*, Pope Francis writes:

> The creation accounts in the Book of Genesis contain, in their own symbolic and narrative language, profound teachings about human existence and its historical reality. They suggest that human life is grounded in three fundamental and closely intertwined relationships: with God, with our neighbour, and with the earth itself.... these three vital relationships have been broken, both outwardly and within us. This rupture is sin. The harmony between the Creator, humanity and creation as a whole was disrupted by our assuming the place of God and refusing to acknowledge our creaturely limitations. This in turn distorted our mandate to "have dominion" over the earth (cf. Genesis 1:28), to "till it and keep it" (Genesis 2:15). As a result the originally harmonious relationship between human beings and nature became conflictual (*LS* 66).

Laudato Si' continues to explore these terms that have so damaged our relationship with the earth. "The term 'dominion' has [wrongly] encouraged the unbridled exploitation of nature ... 'Tilling' refers to cultivation, ploughing and working, while 'keeping' means caring, protecting, overseeing and preserving. This implies a relationship of mutual responsibility between human beings and nature."

Jesus' own relationship with nature gives further insight. Pope Francis concludes his reflection on a scriptural basis for "our care of our common home", by writing of Jesus:

> With moving tenderness [Jesus] would remind them that each one of them is important in God's eyes: "Are not five sparrows sold for two pennies? And not one of them is forgotten before God." ... The Lord was able to invite others to be attentive to the beauty that there is in the world because he himself was in constant touch with nature, lending it attention full of fondness and wonder (*LS* 96, 97).

It is in one of the New Testament letters that we read of God's redemption not of human beings but of all creation. A hymn that would have been sung in the liturgies of the early church is found in Colossians 1. The

Colossians Hymn has the following words, words that are echoed in the statement of faith that we will say in place of our creed this morning:

> [Christ] is the image of the invisible God, the firstborn of all creation; for in him all things in heaven and on earth were created, things visible and invisible, whether thrones or dominions or rulers or powers—all things have been created through him and for him. He himself is before all things, and in him all things hold together. . . . and through him God was pleased to reconcile to himself all things, whether on earth or in heaven, by making peace through the blood of his cross. (Colossians 1:15–20)

One scholar wrote that the words "all things" ring like a bell through the Colossians Hymn, ring like a bell that reminds us beyond all doubt that God has created and loves and redeems all things in creation.

Or as Pope Francis put it,

> Soil, water, mountains: everything is, as it were, a caress of God.

The theologian Elizabeth Johnson, well known for her ground-breaking book *She Who Is* in which she explored female images for God, recently wrote *Creation and Cross: The Mercy of God for a Planet in Peril.* Elizabeth Johnson beautifully articulates the problem for us as we struggle with the need for us to care for this planet in peril:

> I know many people who believe in God's mercy in Christ but find it difficult to connect this faith with the ecological world . . . You can spell out the implications of creation, cross, resurrection, and incarnation all you want, but it feels like a giant seismic shift to rearrange the faith furniture in their head to see that all creatures are embraced by God's mercy.[1]

---

1 Elizabeth A. Johnson, *Creation and Cross: The Mercy of God for a Planet in Peril* (New York: Orbis Books, 2018), p. 198.

Elizabeth Johnson encourages us in reflecting on scripture with the earth in mind in a fascinating way: she asks us to re-imagine the word "us". In this Year of Matthew, we remember Jesus named as Emmanuel, "God with us". The Prologue of John's Gospel says, "The Word became flesh and dwelt among us." Elizabeth Johnson invites us to re-imagine the word "us", to broaden this word, to wonder if it includes not only human beings but all of creation. That God in Christ intentionally came to be with "us", with "all things", as the Colossians Hymn puts it. Elizabeth Johnson writes that we might imagine:

> . . . the round blue earth with humans and all creatures together as a community of creation, and bring this kinship relation to expression in pronouns. . . . our human selves as part of the community of creation, come down from the pinnacle of privilege to rejoin the circle of life, acknowledge the intrinsic value of other creatures, and see their interaction with the living God, then we should be able to include them with ourselves at appropriate moments. So reimagine "us." Try to expand the boundaries of "us" when you think, speak, pray, teach, preach, read, or propose actions, in order to include other creatures along with our human selves in relation to God.[2]

So how might this idea help us when we read the story of the Exodus, the story that we heard this morning of the parting of the Red Sea?

The people of Israel told stories, around campfires, in family groups, eventually writing them down. When they wondered what God is like, one word is all that is needed. Exodus, the reply would have been. Let's tell that story again. The story of the Exodus. There is no better way of shedding light on what God is like. The story of a people enslaved, a people, by God, set free.

What if, encouraged by Elizabeth Johnson, we think not of a people but a planet? What if we imagine the planet enslaved, the planet trapped in a relationship with those who would exploit and neglect her? What if we imagine not a people but a species threatened with extinction? What

---

2 Johnson, *Creation and Cross*, p. 216.

if we imagine that the story of God, hearing, knowing, coming down to save, is about not only the people Israel in Egypt all those years ago, but the planet today, the threatened species today? What if God, who creates and loves and longs to set free, would part the Red Sea to set the planet free, to lead threatened species to the promised land? What if we know that the God of Exodus is at our side as we face this challenge?

Only the trouble is, that if we imagine the story in such a way, we cannot help but realize that Pharoah, the one who enslaves, is, at least, in part, us. When we say that the planet is trapped in a relationship with those who would exploit and neglect her, that relationship is with humanity, with us.

It will not help, though, if we allow ourselves to be overwhelmed with guilt and anxiety and despair about this. It will not help the planet and the species threatened with extinction if we are frozen into inaction. So, how do we spend a little more time treasuring the earth that is our home, spend a little more time praying for its wellbeing; how do we wonder together how we might better care for it?

Once again, Pope Francis is our guide. He writes in *Laudato Si'*:

> We see, increasing sensitivity to the environment and the need to protect nature, along with a growing concern, both genuine and distressing, for what is happening to our planet. Let us review . . . those questions that are troubling us today and which we can no longer sweep under the carpet. Our goal is not to amass information or to satisfy curiosity, but rather to become painfully aware, to dare to turn what is happening in the world to our own personal suffering and thus to discover what each of us can do about it. (*LS* 19)

Accompanied by the creating, loving, forgiving God may we "dare to turn what is happening in the world to our own personal suffering and thus to discover what each of us can do about" bringing healing to the earth.

PART 3

Preaching in the midst of a pandemic

CHAPTER 8

The first Sunday in lockdown—A man called Jesus

Over the last few weeks of Lent, we have heard several of the mighty stories from John's Gospel, seeing in those stories different responses to Jesus. In chapter 3 we saw Nicodemus come to Jesus by night, in the dark, and after a conversation that took place on two different levels, the conversation stayed on two different levels. It was not until Jesus died that Nicodemus, anointing Jesus' body for burial, came into the light. In chapter 4, we saw Jesus encounter a Samaritan woman at Jacob's well. Jesus told her the truth about her life and she, courageously facing that truth, found in Jesus the one who gave her life meaning, who was living water for her, who enabled her to worship in spirit and in truth, the one who enabled her to become a witness to him.

Today, in chapter 9, we hear the story of the man born blind. It could have been, it should have been, a simple encounter. A blind man is given his sight. An imprisoned man is set free. It could have been a simple story. But thanks to the presence of the man's neighbours and the religious leaders it wasn't simple at all:

> As he is walking along, Jesus sees a man blind from birth. His disciples ask him, "Rabbi, who sinned, this man or his parents, that he was born blind?" Jesus answers, "Neither this man nor his parents sinned; he was born blind so that God's works might be revealed in him. We must work the works of him who sent me while it is day; night is coming when no one can work. As long as I am in the world, I am the light of the world." When he has said this, he spits on the ground and makes mud with the saliva

> and spreads the mud on the man's eyes, saying to him, "Go, wash in the pool of Siloam" (which means Sent). Then he goes and washes and comes back able to see. (John 9:1–7)

The man born blind and the man's parents are interrogated by the neighbours and by the religious leaders who cannot see what has happened before their eyes.

> "Then how were your eyes opened?" they ask him. He answers, "The man called Jesus made mud, spread it on my eyes, and said to me, 'Go to Siloam and wash.' Then I went and washed and received my sight." (John 9:10–11)

The man called Jesus, the blind man says.

The religious leaders question the man, and then they question his parents. The healing took place on the sabbath. Trapped in a literal interpretation of the law that was given by God to bring us to life, the leaders cannot see God at work. The man called Jesus must be a sinner. The blind man, pushed further to interpret who it is that has given him his sight, sees a little more clearly. "He is a prophet," he says.

The man's parents, when challenged by the religious leaders are afraid and dodge their questions. "Ask him," they say. And so the Pharisees question the man further. The man will not engage with their rules of law and the breaking of the law. He only knows one thing. "Though I was blind, now I see." He speaks the truth.

The religious leaders challenge the man further and eventually they drive him out of the synagogue. This act matters. He is a person of faith. He has been excluded from the house of faith. This matters and Jesus sees this.

At the opening of the story, Jesus sees the man and reaches out to him. At the end of the story, Jesus sees the man again and reaches out again. The man sees much now. He sees who Jesus is. "Lord, I believe," he says. And he worships him. Through the story the blind man grows in sight. The religious leaders, though, remain blind.

We might feel a little blind ourselves at the moment. Our daily lives, our religious observances, our communities, and the daily lives of every part of the world have been profoundly affected by the spread of a virus that is powerfully contagious and, for some members of our community, deadly. We watch as leaders at all levels struggle to come to grips with fast-changing events and difficult scientific analysis of the best way to act as individuals and communities in response to this change in circumstances. In the Church across the world, leaders with heavy hearts are scaling down and even closing gatherings in church buildings and are looking for creative ways that we might still know ourselves to be the Body of Christ when we cannot be together. This Friday, we announced in the cathedral e-letter that we will not be able to meet for services for a time.

Yes. We might feel a little blind ourselves at the moment.

We might imagine going up to the blind man and asking how it was that he came to see. To see with his physical sight and to see with his spiritual sight. How was it, we might ask, that you came to see . . . and to know then how to live . . . we might ask him.

You know what he is going to say. You know what I am going to say. You can feel it coming. You know what each one of us at the cathedral is going to say and what religious leaders across the world are going to say. For the stones of our beloved cathedral building cry out the words and the music of our beautiful choir, now in recess, sing the words and our very hearts are made to hear the words. Because God made our hearts and wrote on them these words.

How was it that you came to see?

The man called Jesus. The blind man says. Who is it this building bears witness to? The man called Jesus. The man born blind would reply to us, "The man called Jesus made mud, spread it on my eyes, and said to me, 'Go to Siloam and wash.' Then I went and washed and received my sight."

Imagine the intimacy of it. Especially now, when we are not to be so near to one another and we are not to touch our faces. Imagine the intimacy of it.

The man called Jesus will give us our sight even at such a time when it is so very hard to see.

And what shall we see?

Julian of Norwich lived at a time of a plague, a time when many people died, and after a serious illness she saw some things of God, visions that God gave, special sight, if you like, of the way things truly are and especially in difficult times. Julian of Norwich said:

> I did not say that you shall not be tempest tossed, I did not say that you shall not be work weary, I did not say that you shall not be dis-eased; but I did say, You shall not be overcome.

And the reason we shall not be overcome?

The man called Jesus will make mud and spread it on our eyes and tell us to go to Siloam and wash. And he will help us gradually receive our sight.

And we will know that the man called Jesus is with us, and we will know that however tempest-tossed and work-weary and dis-eased we may feel, God is walking alongside us, and we will know that we have the dear company of one another, whether we can literally hold each other's hands, or not.

For the man called Jesus is with us.

We have spent time with some of the mighty stories from John's Gospel this Lent. The mightiest story from that Gospel, the mightiest story in all the Gospels, is yet to come. The Good Friday story. Even this, the strangest of Lenten times, leads us there. This year in churches across the world we do not know, as we usually know, how we shall hear it, how it shall be sung; we cannot see what we can usually see, in what way we shall sit with that story, or how it will transform us. But we do know that it will come and it will be heard and it will transform us. For nothing will stop the man called Jesus from inhabiting our world. Nothing will stop the man called Jesus from dying again and rising again. Nothing will stop the man called Jesus from making mud and spreading it on our eyes and healing our blind eyes that we might see.

CHAPTER 9

Prayer takes courage

Last Tuesday, 12 May, was the 200th anniversary of the birth of Florence Nightingale. Florence Nightingale was infused with what Jesus, in our reading from John 14, called the spirit of truth. The spirit that Jesus promised God would send stands alongside, gives comfort and sheds its fierce loving light on the truth. Florence Nightingale was infused with this spirit as she fought her family and friends to follow her God-given vocation to be a nurse. We might, especially now in this time of pandemic, greatly honour nurses, but in her time, a nurse was viewed with no more respect than a prostitute.

Beyond her famous exploits transforming nursing care for wounded soldiers in Scutari during the Crimean War ... it was in later life that she really transformed healthcare and inspired generations of nurses.[1]

The Lady with the Lamp, as she was known, shed light on the suffering faces of those in her charge, and she also revolutionized the care of patients in hospitals, changing the design and structure of hospitals and their working practices in ways which remain today. The spirit of truth, the spirit of light, also infused the lives of Florence Nightingale's daughters and sons, generations of nurses that followed her path.

Julianne is an Intensive Care nurse in New York City during this time of pandemic:

> All Quiet on the Eastern Front [she writes in an article posted on Facebook]. I am a Covid ICU nurse in New York City, and

---

1 See <https://museumcrush.org/life-beyond-the-lady-of-the-lamp-the-photograph-of-86-year-old-florence-nightingale/>, accessed 29 February 2024.

> yesterday, like many other days lately, I couldn't fix my patient. Sure, that happens all the time in the ICU. It definitely wasn't the first time. It certainly won't be the last. What makes this patient noteworthy? A few things, actually. He was infected with Covid-19, and he lost his battle with Covid-19. He was only 23 years old. I was destroyed by his clinical course in a way that has only happened a few times in my nursing career. It wasn't his presentation. I've seen that before. It wasn't his complications. I've seen that too. It was the grief. It was his parents. The grief I witnessed yesterday, was grief that I haven't allowed myself to recognize since this runaway train got rolling here in early March. I could sense it. It was lingering in the periphery of my mind, but yesterday something in me gave way, and that grief rushed in. I think I was struck by a lot of emotions and realities yesterday. Emotions that have been brewing for weeks, and realities that I have been stifling because I had to in order to do my job effectively. My therapist tells me weekly via Facetime that it's impossible to process trauma when the trauma is still occurring. It just keeps building.[2]

This is only the beginning of Julianne's post, a piece of writing that is relentless, gut-wrenching, woven with the hideous truth that is an Intensive Care Unit in a city where this virus has taken hold.

What is it, this fierce speaking of the truth? Why might we relate it to God's spirit, why might we ponder the possibility that it is infused by God's spirit?

Karl Rahner, a Jesuit theologian, wrote the following about speaking the truth. I read these words a long time ago and they influenced me greatly in my sense of what prayer is. So, I'm sure I've read them to you before. Karl Rahner said:

> When we are feeling lonely—if we are brave enough to resist the urge to call someone up, or go shopping, or take a drug, or

[2] <https://www.wamc.org/post/our-grief-nurses-experience-during-covid-19-pandemic>, accessed 29 February 2024.

> turn to music or TV or go to bed; if we are courageous enough to remain alone and instead of fleeing the pain, to go down into it, we will gradually notice another Presence there, silent, but benevolent and peaceful.[3]

I think he is speaking about sitting with the truth. Telling the truth. Allowing it, pondering it, writing about it, perhaps, as the ICU nurse Julianne has done.

Karl Rahner is talking about not running away from the truth. And he is right to say that this takes courage. Sitting with the truth, be it the pain about which Rahner writes, the trauma about which Julianne writes, be it the fact that we feel trapped in a situation, as we might all do in this pandemic time now, be it some disappointment, or a vague sense that we lack gratitude, be the truth even joy, sitting with the truth takes courage and we would often do anything to avoid it. Rahner knows human nature well, when he catalogues the things that we will turn to, to avoid sitting with the truth—if we are brave enough to resist the urge to call someone up, or go shopping, or take a drug, or turn to music or TV or go to bed; he says. If we are brave enough to pray. Prayer takes courage.

Then Karl Rahner suggests that we will find something in that place where we sit with the truth. He says, we will gradually notice another Presence there, silent, but benevolent and peaceful.

The presence of God. A presence that is usually known gradually, silently. The spirit of truth that Jesus promises. "You know him," Jesus says to the disciples terribly troubled by the truth that he is about to be taken from them. "You know him because he abides with you, and he will be with you" (John 14:17).

There is something more to be said about this presence, this abiding presence. This benevolent peaceful presence will hear us. God will hear us when we speak the truth. This morning's psalm tells us that. "I called to him with my mouth . . . " the psalmist says, "God has heard me, he has heeded the voice of my prayer" (Psalm 66:17,19). God always listens, always hears our cry. Somehow it is when we speak the truth, though,

---

3 Quoted in *Directions*, Newsletter of The Julian Centre, Adelaide, editor, The Revd Philip Carter. Used with permission.

that we sense that, know that we are heard. Notice, as Karl Rahner says, "God's presence, silent, but benevolent and peaceful".

This is Jesus' promise to us, this abiding spirit. The one who bids us tell the truth, pray our truth. What is it we would say in this pandemic time? What is the one thing we would say? About the grief at a world so transformed by virus? About the guilt that we are so fortunate, here? About the worry about what lies ahead, about not knowing what lies ahead? About gratitude, perhaps, for politicians and leaders in so many workplaces, including the church that means so much to us, gratitude for frontline health workers, for nurses, perhaps, nurses like Julianne.

"We stayed while she screamed," Julianne wrote of the mother of her 23-year-old patient just after he died. "We stayed until she finally let go of her vice grip on my hands, her body trembling uncontrollably, as she dissolved into her grief, in the arms of her husband."

"This is ONE patient. One patient, in one ICU, in one hospital, in one city, in one country, on a planet being ravaged by a virus," she wrote.

And this is one nurse's story, one daughter of Florence Nightingale. The one infused with the spirit of truth. The Lady of the Lamp. The light of truth. The truth that holds us, abides with us, in this pandemic time.

CHAPTER 10

We are not alone

She arrived with a very great retinue, with camels bearing spices, and much gold, and precious stones; and she arrived with a mind full of questions. The Queen of Sheba had heard of the wisdom of this Israelite king, King Solomon, and she came to find out about that, to test him out.

As we ponder this reading from 1 Kings 10, I thought we would think about Wisdom in the scriptures, about the questions we might bring to this Wisdom, and I thought we would wonder a little too about what treasures we might bring.

Wisdom in the scriptures is portrayed as a woman, Sophia. We learn about this Wisdom in five books of the Bible: Job, Psalms, Proverbs, Song of Songs and Ecclesiastes, together with two books from the Apocrypha, the Wisdom of Solomon and Sirach. In Proverbs 8 and 9, we hear Wisdom speak:

> Does not wisdom call,
> 	and does not understanding raise her voice?
> On the heights, beside the way,
> 	at the crossroads she takes her stand;
> beside the gates in front of the town,
> 	at the entrance of the portals she cries out:
> "To you, O people, I call,
> 	and my cry is to all that live.
> O simple ones, learn prudence;
> 	acquire intelligence, you who lack it.
> Hear, for I will speak noble things,
> 	and from my lips will come what is right;

for my mouth will utter truth;
wickedness is an abomination to my lips.
All the words of my mouth are righteous;
there is nothing twisted or crooked in them.
They are all straight to one who understands
and right to those who find knowledge.
Take my instruction instead of silver,
and knowledge rather than choice gold;
for wisdom is better than jewels,
and all that you may desire
cannot compare with her." (Proverbs 8:1–11)

In Proverbs, Wisdom is a personification of an aspect of God, the firstborn of God's creative work. Wisdom is God's breath, image, power and spirit, a source of life; an instructor who comes to earth to give wisdom and understanding.[1] Wisdom in the Jewish tradition has three aspects, described by the scholar Richard Harries in this way: "First the divine law given to Moses, laying out the basic principles by which the community is to be guided. Second is the prophetic critique of the people for their failure to live by these rules . . . Third is the divine wisdom—the wisdom both rational and practical, that is reflected in the ordering of the world and from which we can learn by use of our minds and consciences."[2]

Wisdom is found for humankind, in other words, in the law, the laws of ethics grounded in the Ten Commandments, in the urging of the prophets whose poetic voices urge us to abide by that law, and in the beautiful laws of science woven into the universe, human understanding of which is ever evolving. Notice from the passage I read from Proverbs 8 where Wisdom, Sophia, resides:

---

1 See Kate Bruce and Liz Shercliff, *Out of the Shadows: Preaching the Women of the Bible* (London: SCM Press, 2021), p. 4.

2 Richard Harries, *Seeing God in Art* (London: SPCK, 2020), p. 39.

On the heights, beside the way,
at the crossroads she takes her stand;
beside the gates in front of the town,
at the entrance of the portals.

Wisdom lives *on the heights*, the place of pondering, the place where people go to sit with God . . . *beside the way*, as we journey through life . . . *at the crossroads* where decisions of deep significance are made . . . *beside the gates in front of the town*, in the thick of things, the political world, the world of business, the bustle of things.

So, as the Queen of Sheba did, we bring to Wisdom our questions. In the midst of a coronavirus pandemic, for example, we bring questions, questions of healing, management and meaning. The scientists work with the questions of healing for us. Devoting their lives to an engagement with the wisdom woven into the laws that govern the universe, scientists like Oxford-based Dame Sarah Gilbert, who worked to discover the AstraZeneca vaccine, ask questions that lead to vaccines and treatments. Our gratitude for this work done so speedily on our behalf is profound. Did you hear the story of an enthusiastic Centre Court crowd at Wimbledon, who gave Dame Sarah Gilbert a spontaneous standing ovation when she was welcomed to the Royal Box in a heart-warming start to the Championship?

And then there are the questions of management. Standing beside the gate in front of the town, Wisdom, Sophia, guides politicians, health professionals, police, media, as they seek to chart the safest way for communities to control the virus, yet still to live in some sort of freedom. Working with a virus which we are only beginning to understand, and which is evolving as we do so, the prophets, those who speak Sophia's voice, might well urge us to look graciously on those who devote their lives to such a struggle. We have only to look at the worn faces of the politicians who speak to us day by day, to know that their struggle with Wisdom born on behalf of those they serve is torrid.

The toughest questions are questions of meaning. We read of a mother in Sydney just after she had given birth to her child, dying of Covid. I read to you on Easter Day the words of an ICU nurse in New York City, overwhelmed by the grief of the parents of a patient in his twenties who lost his fight with Covid. We see images of long rows of graves in Brazil where Covid is out of control. We can barely articulate our questions in the face of such suffering. Sometimes our questions to Sophia, Wisdom, God, are more like images, images we have seen in the news, images etched on our minds . . . sometimes our questions seem only to find their home in silence. Silence, as we sit and wonder.

In the New Testament, Jesus is portrayed as Wisdom. The prologue to John's Gospel calls Jesus the Word of God. We might also say the Wisdom of God.

> In the beginning was the Word, and the Word was with God, and the Word was God. He was in the beginning with God. All things came into being through him, and without him not one thing came into being. What has come into being in him was life, and the life was the light of all people. The light shines in the darkness, and the darkness did not overcome it. (John 1:1–5)

Words about Jesus the Word and Wisdom of God.

When we wonder about the questions we have in times of awful suffering, it may be that it is to Jesus and his struggle we turn. For there are times when questions do not have answers. There are times, I think, when we need to sit with questions. Perhaps the most poignant question ever uttered is that of Jesus on his cross: "My God, My God, why have you forsaken me?" Reflecting on Jesus dying on the cross, a former Dean of Westminster Abbey, Michael Mayne, wrote, "What Good Friday does is invite us once again to open ourselves to the God who doesn't answer our Job-like questions about the 'Why?' of evil and pain and suffering: instead, he enters into the heart of the questions himself. The crucified Jesus is the only accurate picture of God the world has ever seen."[3] Jesus, Wisdom, strangely enters into the heart of the questions. Sometimes, yes, we can only sit with questions, knowing that Wisdom is our companion.

I read a little while ago these verses from Proverbs:

---

3 Michael Mayne, *Dust that Dreams of Glory* (London: Canterbury Press, 2017), p. 60.

> Take my instruction instead of silver,
>   and knowledge rather than choice gold;
> for wisdom is better than jewels,
>   and all that you may desire cannot compare with her.

The Queen of Sheba must have sensed this. She sought King Solomon out with camels bearing spices, a great amount of gold and precious stones. What shall we bring, as we come to God, Jesus, Wisdom, with our questions, whatever they might be this night? What shall we bring? It might be that we bring gifts of money, time, prayer. It might be that what God treasures most, sees most as precious, is our coming at all. Our trusting God with our questions. Our giving of ourselves to Wisdom's presence. Our faith in the One who sometimes does not answer our questions at all, but helps us know that, with the questions that in our time and place seem to have no answer, we are not alone.

CHAPTER 11

What is God like?

"What is God like?" we might sometimes wonder to ourselves, especially when the world changes so unexpectedly. "What is God like? . . . and how would God have us be?"

A few weeks ago, I mentioned one of my favourite authors, Rowan Williams, thinking about this question. His advice was to steer away from definitions and descriptions and concepts. His advice was, instead, to tell stories. Only a whole story could begin to give us insight into God.

The people of Israel told stories, around campfires, in family groups, eventually writing them down. What is God like? One word is all that is needed. Exodus, the reply would have been. Let's tell that story again. The story of the Exodus. There is no better way of shedding light on what God is like. The story of a people enslaved, a people, set free by God.

So, we begin this Sunday by dipping into this story, the story of the Exodus, the one story, if only one was allowed, which tells of who God is in the faith of the people Israel, the faith in which Jesus lived his life. The word "exodus" means "journey out of". "Ex" means out, exit, for example, "od" means journey. Exodus, a journey out of slavery. The story meant so much that, in the written version, the telling of it is interrupted with instructions for a liturgy to remember it, the liturgy for the Passover.

Joseph's family, at the end of the story of Genesis, were settled in Egypt, thriving, growing in numbers, until the Egyptians felt threatened by them. The king Pharaoh, who did not know about Joseph, decided to oppress the Israelite people with forced labour and to have their first-born sons killed. It was into this situation that a baby boy was born to a man and a woman from the house of Levi.

> When his mother could hide him no longer, she got a papyrus basket for him, and plastered it with bitumen and pitch; she put the child in it and placed it among the reeds on the bank of the river. The daughter of Pharaoh came down to bathe at the river, while her attendants walked beside the river. She saw the basket among the reeds and sent her maid to bring it. When she opened it, she saw the child. He was crying, and she took pity on him. (Exodus 2:3–6)

And she named him Moses because she "drew him out" of the water.

God does not appear in the first two chapters of the story. God appears in the third chapter when the people in slavery cry out and God sees and hears the pain of the people, and God knows their suffering and comes down to deliver the people and lead them out—through Moses—whose name, remember, means "to draw out".

The story Exodus tells of this journey out, this longing of God to set free, the story of the ten plagues and the parting of the Red Sea, the setbacks, the grumbling in the difficult conditions of wilderness, the giving of the manna and the quails, the instructions given on the mountaintop for living well, the journey to the Promised Land.

This journey out was not easy and in the midst of this book we see what happens when waiting for God is too hard. The story of the golden calf shows that we easily tire of waiting for God; we turn instead to worship gods of our own making. When Moses took too long talking with God on the mountain, the people of Israel made a calf of gold, and they worshipped that instead. This story Exodus tells the story of God and the story of human nature all woven in together.

The worship of other gods was something with which Jesus was not unfamiliar. Our reading from Matthew 16 is set at Caesarea Philippi, about 20 miles north of the Sea of Galilee. Caesarea Philippi had a history as a place of worship of gods. A Baal centre of worship, it became known as Paneas when the god Pan was worshipped there in a famous grotto and spring. The Roman Herod the Great had the place renamed Caesarea Philippi, after he built a temple there to Caesar Augustus. This place had strong associations with Jewish and pagan nationalistic and religious rituals. The worship of other gods. What better place for Jesus to ask his question, the question about his identity:

> Who do people say that the Son of Man is? (Matthew 16:13)

This is the turning point of the Gospel story. It is a story written for the Jewish context and so allusions are often given to the Old Testament stories. The story of Jesus' birth is told in Matthew's Gospel; his baptism, his teaching on mountains is told in five sections, reminiscent of the five books of the Torah. It is unmistakable that Jesus is being portrayed as a new Moses in this Gospel. And then, in the scene at Caesarea Philippi, Jesus turns to face the journey to Jerusalem. But before he goes, he needs that motley band of disciples who have accompanied him to begin to understand who he is. And who they are as well.

> Who do people say that the Son of Man is?
> Some say John the Baptist, but others Elijah, and still
> others Jeremiah or one of the prophets.
> But who do you say that I am? (Matthew 16:13–15)

Peter, who we know will leap out bravely into the unknown, speaks words in which he probably just glimpses an understanding . . .

> You are the Messiah, the Son of the living God. (Matthew 16:16)

Peter senses in Jesus something about his closeness to God, his living as the one who called God "Abba", his teaching and healing and spending time with them all coming from Jesus' knowing God in a way that was different from any other religious person they had known. This "Son of Man" is a human being unlike even the prophets of long ago. This Jesus is somehow about God breaking in, the living God whose very nature is Exodus, who leads the people from any sort of slavery to a freedom that only God knows . . . breaking in. The only word that was available in the language of Peter's faith, the only word that seemed to be close to all this was "Messiah".

Peter then gets more than he bargained for. He thought he was exploring Jesus' identity. But he found that in doing that he was given his own. After the revelation of his identity, this new Moses, this Messiah, Jesus, then blesses, names and commissions Peter:

> Blessed are you, Simon son of Jonah! For flesh and blood has not revealed this to you, but my Father in heaven. And I tell you, you are Peter, and on this rock I will build my church, and the gates of Hades will not prevail against it. I will give you the keys of the kingdom of heaven, and whatever you bind on earth will be bound in heaven, and whatever you loose on earth will be loosed in heaven. (Matthew 16:17–19)

Only God could have opened Peter's eyes to who Jesus was. We can only wonder what it was like for Jesus to hear the friend he knew to be so impulsive, so flawed, name him so. We do know that Jesus blesses him and points out to him that this insight is God-given. And it is on the one, however flawed, however impulsive, who sees and names, identifies Jesus, that his church will be built. Jesus names Peter, gives him his identity as the Rock, the foundation of the church that Jesus will build. A church that Jesus promises will never be prevailed against. A church in which Jesus' presence nurtures us in living as he did, as the ones who call God "Abba". A church in which Jesus' presence nurtures our teaching and healing and spending time with one another as the "Son of Man" did when he walked the earth. A church that, at its best, accompanies all who enter its doors across time and space, as Jesus accompanies all who would follow him. A church that whatever it faces, will, as Jesus said to Peter, never be prevailed against. For Jesus is the Son of the God of Exodus. Exodus. The journey out of.

We would love to journey out of this time, wouldn't we? We would love to think that all the effort we have put in to isolating and hand sanitizing and even not singing when we love to sing, all the little things we have done, will soon lead us through. We would love to know the vaccine is on its way and that will bring this to an end. The story of Exodus tells us that this "journeying out" can be long and difficult and that we human beings will struggle terribly with it at times.

"What is God like?" we might sometimes wonder to ourselves, especially when the world changes so unexpectedly. "What is God like? . . . and how would God have us be?"

God is like the story of Exodus, the scriptures tell us, and we . . . we are the church. A place and people where the story is told. A place where our grumbling and our worshipping of other gods is forgiven. A place where we are fed with manna from heaven, the bread of life. A place and people named and commissioned and blessed by Jesus who lived so closely to this God of Exodus that he trusted him even with the greatest exodus, the greatest "journeying out", the giving of his life.

We are the church. A place and people in whose company we might dare to hear Jesus say to us, "Who do you say that I am?" . . . and in pondering our answer we might, to our surprise, hear Jesus speaking our names.

CHAPTER 12

An extraordinary truth

George Frideric Handel, in his most loved oratorio *Messiah*, opens the third and final part with the soprano singing the glorious aria, "I know that my redeemer liveth".

That, I think, is why we have entered our cathedral today. We know that our redeemer liveth. We know, or, perhaps, we long to know, we have heard it said, it has caused us to wonder. Could it possibly be? That our redeemer liveth? We have walked through Holy Week with Jesus and kept company with his fear and courage and his cruel death. We have watched him cry out to his Father God, a God he experienced this one time as absent, we have seen him forgive those who nailed him to his cross and we have heard him hand, into his Father's hands, his spirit, as he breathed his final breath. We have watched his broken body being taken down from the cross and we have seen it laid in the tomb. And yesterday, on Holy Saturday, this day sometimes referred to as a grey day, we have waited.

And then we have come, come to see, to hear, to spend time with the possibility. The possibility of the extraordinary truth. That our redeemer liveth.

There is only one place to know this truth. To sense its possibility. To glimpse its wonder. Only one place. And that is the place of death. Over the coming weeks, we will hear the stories of our redeemer living. It will always be in the dead places. Today it is the tomb and Mary, Mary searching for his body, just to spend time with him, to say farewell again. Next week, we will gather in the upper room in the midst of the disciples' fear and Thomas' doubt. Another time it is the Emmaus Road, where the disciples are all questions and confusion. Then, there is Peter, fishing where there are no fish, and only the echo of three denials and the crowing of the cock and guilt. Oh, the guilt. Jesus comes to all these places, all our dark places, all our dead places.

We've known some of those this year, haven't we?

During this year of pandemic, we know, those of us who live on Australian shores, that we are the lucky ones. Yet even we know that our world has entered a dark place from which we may never quite recover. Other parts of the world have not been so fortunate. There are tombs everywhere. Tombs filled with the dead this disease has taken, filled with dreams destroyed, families pushed to limits unknown until they found themselves living together alone for months on end, the education of children and young adults stunted, economies battered by lockdowns and uncertainty. We knew from very early on that the healthcare workers were the ones who would hold us until they almost broke. We heard in a sermon, on the 200th anniversary of Florence Nightingale's birth, the voice of one of her daughters. Her voice shall be our tomb, this Easter morning.

Julianne is an Intensive Care nurse in New York City during this time of pandemic:

> All Quiet on the Eastern Front [she writes in an article posted on Facebook]. I am a Covid ICU nurse in New York City, and yesterday, like many other days lately, I couldn't fix my patient. . . . He was infected with Covid-19, and he lost his battle with Covid-19. He was only 23 years old. I was destroyed by his clinical course in a way that has only happened a few times in my nursing career . . . It was the grief. It was his parents. The grief I witnessed yesterday, was grief that I haven't allowed myself to recognize since this runaway train got rolling here in early March . . . .[1]

This is only the beginning of Julianne's post, a piece of writing that is relentless, gut-wrenching, woven with the hideous truth that is an Intensive Care Unit in a city where this virus has taken hold. A crying

1 <https://www.wamc.org/post/our-grief-nurses-experience-during-covid-19-pandemic>, accessed 29 February 2024.

out almost like Jesus' crying out. "My God, my God, why have you forsaken me?" A cross, where death seems relentless and only to be borne. A tomb, filled with the deaths that the coronavirus has wrought. Jesus died, crucified, death by asphyxiation, literally *being unable to breathe*. Covid deaths are not unlike Jesus' death in a way, death by being *unable to breathe*.

This tomb holds nurse Julianne's story; what is ours?

Where do we need him? Is it beside our tombs as it was for Mary, the place where we need to sit with something, someone, lost to death, a view of the world no longer real, perhaps? Or, are we more like the disciples in that upper room, frightened by it all, *this all*, this year, doubting even a world we thought we knew, let alone the possibility of God, of Jesus alive? Or are we just baffled, walking on our Emmaus roads, trying to make some sense of the stories of this pandemic year? Or is it guilt, is there something we have done, some way we have been we cannot shake? We wonder how he could possibly forgive us for we surely cannot forgive ourselves. Where shall the risen redeemer who liveth meet us, speak our names in his oh so surprising, living voice?

What is he saying to us, wherever he meets us, wherever we need him most? *I am with you*. You thought I was destroyed, didn't you; you thought Covid-19 would finish me off; you thought your sin would send me away, was that it? What is he saying to us?

When, like Mary, we barely recognize him in the early morning light.

Our names.

As we look at him so puzzled, he says our names.

The words that mean *us*, to him, as we are, loved and forgiven and now bathed in hope. This redeemer that liveth *says our names*. That's all he needs to do, really. For then we'll know. That the fear or the confusion or the guilt or the grief, whatever it is—is known and held and kept company with. Is not enough to send him away disappointed in us, disgusted in us, perhaps. Is not enough to destroy him and God's love.

It's our names we will hear. And then we will recognize him and know. Know what the very walls of our cathedral cry out. Know what the windows and the reredos tell, what the scriptures say and the choir sings. Know what our beloved organ plays. Know.

That our redeemer liveth. That Jesus lives. That, whatever our time and place might tell us will bring life to its knees, will not be the end. As the dawn rises each Easter Day, this Easter Day, we will know again, through the speaking of our names. Jesus lives. Our redeemer liveth.

CHAPTER 13

God is always arriving

> O that you would tear open the heavens and come down . . .

The prophet Isaiah cries out to God.

> O that you would tear open the heavens and come down . . .

On this Sunday, Advent Sunday, and all through this season when our cathedral is dressed in purple, the prophets are our poets, the writers of our prayers. The prophets express our longings and Advent is the time for sitting with longing. For woven into that for which we long is the voice of God. Woven into the prophets' voice is the cry of humanity for God's presence. The prophet articulates the conversation between us and God. And woven into the prophet's voice is a stark and honest confession of what it is to be human. How we try and how we fail. How we thrive and how we fall apart. How the challenges of living in a physical and finite world at times enliven us and at other times bring us to our knees.

It has been said in so many circumstances and in so many ways. Last Advent Sunday we *could not have known* what lay ahead for the world. We could not have pondered the existence of a virus that would take its sinister and deadly hold. We could not have seen a world in which we would experience a week like last week, when one day all in our state was cautious optimism, and three days later we were confined to our homes, allowed out only for essential supplies and not even for a walk. And yet we know we are the lucky ones. We wake each morning to news stories showing healthcare workers across the world, their heads in their hands, "stressing out, striving and even dying in alarming numbers on the Covid front line",[1] to quote one online newspaper. We wake each morning to Covid statistics that make us shudder in horror. We are the lucky ones and *we* are rattled by this.

And so we remember that in Advent we look to the prophets to speak on our behalf:

> O that you would tear open the heavens and come down,
> so that the mountains would quake at your presence –
> as when fire kindles brushwood
> and the fire causes water to boil –
> to make your name known to your adversaries,
> so that the nations might tremble at your presence! (Isaiah 64:1–2)

Isaiah opens this passage expressing our longing for God's presence, God's action, God's healing, and then the prophet speaks of us. Confesses, really, about us. Tells the harsh truth of what it is to be . . . us:

> But you were angry, and we sinned;
> because you hid yourself, we transgressed.
> We have all become like one who is unclean,
> and all our righteous deeds are like a filthy cloth.
> We all fade like a leaf,
> and our iniquities, like the wind, take us away. (Isaiah 64:5–6)

The prophet knows about prayer. Knows how we must address God. Prayer needs confession, needs a deep honesty about who we are and how we are. Prayer needs to come from the truth.

Also, prayer needs to glimpse the one to whom, in whom, we pray. We cannot see God, and so we need the prophet's poetry. The prophet uses, in this passage, the image of a potter for this.

> O LORD, you are our Father;
> we are the clay, and you are our potter;
> we are all the work of your hand . . . (Isaiah 64:8)

---

1 *Guardian*, 25 November 2020.

The prophet knows about prayer. Prayer needs to come from the truth.

The writer C. S. Lewis put it this way. He speaks of our attempts at prayer:

> The attempt is not to escape from space and time and from my creaturely situation as a subject facing objects. It is more modest: to re-awake the awareness of that situation. If that can be done, there is no need to go anywhere else. This situation itself is, at every moment, a possible theophany. Here is the holy ground; the Bush is burning now.
>
> Of course this attempt may be attended with almost every degree of success or failure. The prayer preceding all prayers is, "May it be the real I who speaks. May it be the real Thou that I speak to."
>
> It is more modest: to re-awake the awareness of [our creaturely] situation. If that can be done, there is no need to go anywhere else. This situation itself is, at every moment, a possible theophany. Here is the holy ground; the Bush is burning now.[2]

Jesus, in this morning's reading from this year's Gospel of Mark, is saying a similar thing. He is speaking about the Son of Man coming and he uses all sorts of strange language, but in the end he is clear about us and what we are to do—he says, simply, really, to us, "Keep awake." There is to be an arrival, there is to be a profound change. He urges us to work and to watch. A devout Jew, Jesus has learnt from the prophets, he uses language as a prophet does. He exhorts us to watch as, for example, we might watch nature changing:

> From the fig tree learn its lesson: as soon as its branch becomes tender and puts forth its leaves, you know that summer is near. So also, when you see these things taking place, you know that he is near, at the very gates. (Mark 13:28–9)

---

2 C. S. Lewis, *Letters to Malcolm: Chiefly on Prayer* (New York: Harcourt, 1964), pp. 81–2.

There is to be an arrival, there is to be a profound change.

Jesus uses another image.

It is as if, he says, a man is going on a journey, and he puts his slaves in charge, each with his work, and commands the doorkeeper to be on the watch. But they do not know when the master of the house will come home, in the evening, or at midnight, or at cockcrow, or at dawn, and he may find them asleep when he comes suddenly. In this story, Jesus has us feel the urgency, the necessity of keeping awake.

There is to be an arrival, there is to be a profound change.

All we are to do is to weave our lives with prayer. So, let's look a little more at what C. S. Lewis says. Jesus says "Keep awake." It is his Advent exhortation. C. S. Lewis tells us

> to re-awake . . .
>
> to re-awake the awareness of [our creaturely] situation. If that can be done, there is no need to go anywhere else. This situation itself is, at every moment, a possible theophany. Here is the holy ground; the Bush is burning now.

Wherever we are is the place to pray. In the stuff of prayer.

> Here is the holy ground; the Bush is burning now.

And beautifully, C. S. Lewis says we are to pray in this way:

> The prayer preceding all prayers is, "May it be the real I who speaks. May it be the real Thou that I speak to."

No games, no trying to make ourselves what we are not. No trying to imagine what God is not. We long for the real Thou. But God longs too. God longs for the real us.

> "May it be the real I who speaks. May it be the real Thou that I speak to."

Each year we begin again, tell the story again. Each year we reflect on our story held in God's story. We look back at a year unfolded and we look ahead, knowing that the following year will have its place in God's creating, redeeming love. Each year we allow the prophets to speak for us, to hear Jesus remind us to keep awake, to pray.

Each year in Advent we imagine waiting for an arriving. But our longing for God is written on our hearts. God was here before us, do you see? God is always arriving. The one we exhort to tear open the heavens and come down is with us. Or as C. S. Lewis wrote, "Here is the holy ground; the Bush is burning now."

PART 4

Through the eyes of artists

CHAPTER 14

Thin places

I wonder if it was like a Clarice Beckett painting, the ascension, I mean. I wonder if it was like one of Clarice Beckett's paintings in the exhibition entitled *The Present Moment* showing in our Art Gallery. A friend told me about the paintings after she saw them at the gallery, and so I wanted to see for myself. My friend said that you couldn't see the boundaries between things, the paintings were so misty it was difficult to see where one thing ended and the next began. So I wondered if the paintings might be a little like the ascension, the day when Jesus, the resurrected Jesus, left the earth and went to be with his God:

> "A little while, and you will no longer see me, and again a little while, and you will see me." [Jesus says, when he is talking to the disciples as they walk towards the garden after their final supper together.] The disciples wonder, "What does he mean by saying to us, 'A little while, and you will no longer see me, and again a little while, and you will see me'", "What does he mean by this 'a little while'? We do not know what he is talking about." Jesus knows that they want to ask him, so he says to them, "Are you discussing among yourselves what I meant when I said, 'A little while, and you will no longer see me, and again a little while, and you will see me'? Very truly, I tell you, you will weep and mourn, but the world will rejoice; you will have pain, but your pain will turn into joy." (John 16:16–20)

It was after the resurrection appearances that he left them for good. He came to them in such different ways, just as they needed him, really, in the resurrection. He said Mary's name by the tomb, and he brought peace to the disciples frightened in the upper room. He showed Thomas his hands and his side; and, Peter, he forgave Peter by the charcoal fire. He came to them just as they needed him. It was after the appearances that he led the disciples as far as Bethany and, lifting up his hands, he blessed them and while he was blessing them, he was carried up into heaven, so Luke's Gospel says.

> "A little while, and you will no longer see me, and again a little while, and you will see me."

Jesus said this in our reading from John's Gospel tonight. This was true. They lost him as he died and then they saw him again in the resurrection. They did weep and mourn and then their pain did turn into joy, a mysterious joy, admittedly. And then, he left them again, carried up into heaven as he blessed them. This time, they did not seem engulfed in sadness, they did not seem to weep and mourn. This time they seemed almost at home with his departure.

I went to the Art Gallery and I looked at the Clarice Beckett paintings. My favourite ones were of sunsets by the sea. It's like that in an exhibition, don't you think? There are so many paintings, and so you find one or two that seem to reach out to you, and then you sit with those one or two. So, for me, it was the sunsets by the sea. In one of the paintings there was a figure, a person. The painting was so misty that I couldn't tell much about them, but they were walking away from me, walking on the sand. The sand blurred into the sea and then the sea blurred into the sky. In the sky was a beautiful, gentle, soft orange sun. All the colours in the Clarice Beckett paintings were soft. It was as if the figure was walking, guided by the gentle orange light of the setting sun. I did wonder if the ascension might be just like this painting. Jesus seeing God, like the gentle orange sun, knowing his time had come to leave the earth, leave his human life, fixed in a time and a place, and be with God. I wondered if for the disciples watching it hadn't been as mysterious as this painting. Where the boundaries weren't clear at all. As if really the boundaries didn't matter. As if the separation between sand and sea and sky didn't matter. As Jesus was ascending to his Father, what might have seemed like an awful wrench wasn't at all, because the boundaries weren't clear, perhaps?

In Celtic spirituality, the writers speak about "thin places", where the boundaries between earth and heaven aren't clear. Margaret Silf, who writes about Celtic spirituality, put it this way:

> For the Celts there was never any shadow of doubt that these two worlds, the visible and the invisible, the material and the spiritual, were one. In every way the visible and the invisible were interwoven, as surely as the air we breathe and the food we eat come together to give life to our bodies. The invisible was separated from our sense perceptions only by the permeable membrane of consciousness. Sometimes that membrane could seem as solid as a brick wall. Sometimes it could be very thin. Indeed, we speak even today of some places being as "thin places", meaning that the presence of the invisible and the spiritual in those places is almost palpable.[1]

The ascension of Jesus was a thin place. The disciples sensed this, reassured perhaps by his closeness to them in the resurrection. Jesus came and went in his earthly life with the disciples; came and went when he ministered to them and then disappeared up his mountain to pray alone; came and went when he died on the cross; came and went when he appeared resurrected and then ascended into heaven. It was the way of him. But by the time the ascension of Jesus happened it was almost as if the disciples knew, knew in the thinness of that place, knew that the boundary between earth and heaven was like a whisper and they needn't be troubled by his disappearances anymore. Yes. The ascension of Jesus was a thin place. Perhaps the ascension of Jesus is *the* thin place.

We might have our own thin places. Places in nature where we know we can just sit, and without our needing to struggle to pray, God sometimes seems close. For me the nearest place is Encounter Bay. Just sitting, watching the gentle waves roll in, and the birds fossick and fly, and the smell of seaweed and just once in a while a sea urchin, those round shells in red or green or purple or white, almost seem to call out to me

---

1 Margaret Silf, *Sacred Spaces: Stations on a Celtic Way* (Brewster, MA: Paraclete Press, 2001), p. 9.

from the midst of that seaweed. And all I need to do is sit and watch the gentle waves. Every now and then the boundaries between earth and heaven don't seem clear at all. Every now and then one might almost say that God is close.

Was the ascension like that I wonder? Like the places where God is closest to us? Like a Clarice Beckett painting that is so misty that I couldn't tell much about the figure in it, but they were walking away from me, walking on the sand. The sand blurs into the sea and then the sea blurs into the sky. In the sky is a beautiful, gentle, soft orange sun. It is as if the figure is walking guided by the gentle orange light of the setting sun.

The disciples weren't troubled when Jesus left them this time, when he ascended to be with God. When we are fortunate to find peace in our thin places, perhaps, we might notice that we are not troubled either.

CHAPTER 15

Revolution not comfort

We sometimes think of her as demure. "Hail Mary Full of Grace", our choir sang as the Introit to this Choral Evensong devoted to her memory. We sometimes think of her as quiet, gentle, clothed in blue, possibly with a halo. Gazing at her newborn child in the swaddling bands in that manger, or later in the story . . . holding his crucified body in her arms. We sometimes think of her as passive. But I'm not so sure about that.

The Archbishop of Canterbury, Justin Welby, speaking at the Lambeth Conference, said this:

> The Church is a place of revolution without violence, called to set the world the right way up.

And he described Mary's Song, the Magnificat, as "a statement of revolution not comfort . . . the statement of a revolutionary".

We sing Mary's song, the Magnificat, each Sunday evening at Choral Evensong. Different settings by different composers, each shining light on a different interpretation of Mary's words to her cousin Elizabeth, spoken soon after she found out that she was pregnant. Mary visited Elizabeth, who was herself six months pregnant, to share her news with her. Have we thought of that as we have sung, listened to, the Magnificat, as Mary speaks of her soul magnifying the Lord . . . have we thought of Mary as the speaker of the statement of a revolutionary?

We first meet Mary in the Gospel accounts in the story of the annunciation, the meeting of the Angel Gabriel with Mary as told in the Gospel of Luke, as we heard in our second reading this evening. Gabriel encounters Mary and asks her a question. *Will you help to set the world the right way up?* might be one way of phrasing the question, using Justin

Welby's words. Mary engages robustly with the angel. She is frightened, ... we know that because Gabriel tells her not to be afraid. And she wrestles with what she is being asked to do ... she ponders, gives weight to, Gabriel's request. Mary shows great courage in this encounter, courage in the face of her quite reasonable fear.

This story has been portrayed in art over the centuries, and I wonder if something of Mary's radical nature can be found in the text and, perhaps, in artists' portrayal of this story. My favourite painting of the meeting of Gabriel with Mary is found in the National Gallery in London. The artist is Fra Filippo Lippi.

A number of years ago, we went on a holiday to England and I returned with a treasure, as one often does on holiday. This treasure was a book. We visited the National Gallery in London and there this book caught my eye. It is called *Painting the Word.* Its subtitle is *Christian Pictures and their Meanings*, and it is written by a priest and biblical scholar, a former Dean of Christ Church, Oxford, John Drury. The book opens exploring paintings about gazing—in a chapter entitled "Kind regards", John Drury spends time with paintings that have subjects regarding, gazing at, something of meaning and then he follows the story of Christ's nativity, baptism, ministry, passion and resurrection—all through paintings, paintings from one particular gallery in one particular city, the National Gallery in London.

John Drury devotes part of his chapter on the annunciation to the painting that I love with that title by Fra Filippo Lippi, which was painted in the middle of the fifteenth century. Fra Filippo Lippi's *Annunciation* explores Mary's question to Gabriel "How can this be?" The painter has the audacity, really, to illustrate his idea of the answer to Mary's question "How can this be?" How can it be that Mary, a virgin, can conceive and bear in her womb a son? How can it be that Mary, a young woman, can help to set the world the right way up? We know well Gabriel's answer to her question:

> The Holy Spirit will come upon you, and the power of the Most High will overshadow you ... For nothing is impossible with God. (Luke 1:35,37)

Fra Filippo Lippi shows us in his painting how he thinks this miracle takes place. The painting is in two parts. On the left we find Gabriel in an enclosed garden, outside the house, kneeling in conversation with Mary who is seated on the right side in a courtyard. They speak across a low wall, placed on the wall is a vase of lilies, lilies for Mary. At the back of the painting are the bottom steps of a staircase leading upwards. The staircase leads to God. John Drury explains:

> From the middle of a cloud, [at the top of a staircase], representing the overshadowing in the text, God's hand reaches down in blessing, dispatching the dove which drops steeply down the staircase to the level of Mary's womb.[1]

> The dove is closer to Mary's body than is customary in Annunciation pictures—it was usually put in the air above her head—and there is a new intimacy. [The dove hovers close to Mary's body.] But there is still a gap. What happens there? The answer will resolve Mary's great question "How?"
>
> Careful inspection [of the painting] reveals a spray of golden particles issuing from the dove's beak. At their centre, one little jet of them carries forward horizontally and meets—contact at last!—an answering spray [of golden particles] from Mary's womb issuing through a tiny slit in her [dress]."[2]

Fra Filippo Lippi illustrates the answer to Mary's question "How?" in his painting. Visually, he shows how the incarnation is done. God's Spirit, pictured as a dove sends God's question to Mary in golden particles of light. Mary's reply, more golden particles of light, is pictured by the painter as emitting from her womb. Mary's "Let it be with me according to your word" meets God's request. God is made incarnate in the world through this encounter. God asks a young girl, "Will you?" and she replies "Yes." It is a two-way conversation. The painting suggests that Mary's role in the incarnation is of the same significance as the role of

---

1 John Drury, *Painting the Word* (London: Yale University Press, 1999), p. 49.

2 Drury, *Painting the Word*, p. 52.

God. Mary's courage that day met with God's longing to set the world the right way up. And the Word was made flesh and dwelt among us, full of grace and truth. After all, Jesus' mother was full of grace and truth.

Mary spoke of God's longing for the healing of creation in the words of the Magnificat, those words of "revolution not comfort". As she speaks these words, Mary identifies herself with the lowly, foreshadowing the raising up of the lowly and the fulfilment of God's promises in her son Jesus. She speaks of God's redeeming work, not to happen in the future but as having already been fulfilled.

> And his mercy is on them that fear him: throughout all generations.
> He hath shewed strength with his arm:
> he hath scattered the proud in the imagination of their hearts.
> He hath put down the mighty from their seat: and
>   hath exalted the humble and meek.
> He hath filled the hungry with good things: and
>   the rich he hath sent empty away.

Her faith is such that she believes God's "turning the world the right way up" is already being acted out. And acted out in a new way. As one scholar put it:

> The overthrow of the powerful has not come about through the mounting up of the weak in rebellion but through the weakness of a child. [The Magnificat] describes the dramatic reversal that is the signature of God's acts. . . . And more than predictions of what is to come, the Magnificat praises God for the goodness of God's nature and redemption.[3]

Mary, a young girl of extraordinary courage, deep faith in God. A young girl, whose life is surely steeped in the scriptures, for the Magnificat owes much to Hannah's song, lives out that faith in her response to God. A

---

3 R. Alan Culpepper, *The Gospel of Luke*, New Interpreter's Bible (Nashville, TN: Abingdon Press, 1995), p. 55.

young girl who helped set the world the right way up. May we pray that she be with us, in the words of the beautiful aria that was sung this night:

> Turn then, our advocate,
> your eyes of mercy towards us.
> And after this our exile
> show to us the blessed fruit of your womb,
> Jesus.
> Merciful, holy, sweet virgin Mary.

CHAPTER 16

Reflections on a grey puddle beside a cathedral

The photo in our Evensong booklets was taken by John Hamilton, one Friday morning after the early service in the Lady Chapel, after the congregation had had its breakfast together. There was a puddle in the cathedral car park and, in the puddle, a reflection of the cathedral. Autumn leaves were dotted around the puddle, adding colour to the grey of the asphalt and of the cathedral stone. And John took his photo of this: the cathedral's reflection in the puddle, the autumn leaves scattered around.

I wondered about that. About the greyness of things and what light does. Light reflecting the truth of a building that points to the most profound truth. You can see the spires of the cathedral in the reflection in the puddle. The spires, pointing to the heavens, are reflected in the grey puddle so bounded on the earth. The building pointing to the truth of God, God who creates all things, God who redeems all things too. And the building that speaks of these things. Speaks to all of us who enter its doors. To all of us who call it home, to all who enter on occasion, and to all who walk through the doors for the very first time.

The former dean of Westminster Abbey, Michael Mayne, wrote this about the Abbey he served:

> I never fail to be moved by how affected [visitors] are by the atmosphere in this historic, holy and storied space. Although I

> use words with which to tell its story, it is invariably the space that speaks.[1]

For us, too, it is often the space that speaks. On this, our Patronal Festival, on the feast day for our patron St Peter, we might think about the building and what it means to us and what it means to God. We might think about Peter.

The grey puddle might be a symbol of Peter, in a way. He is so flawed. Always impetuous. Always blundering into things. So often dominated by fear rather than the love he so longs to express. Rushing out on the sea to be with Jesus after he had calmed a storm, and then looking down in terror at the waves and sinking . . . until Jesus grabs his hands, saying "O ye of little faith." Rushing to name him "Messiah" at Caesarea Philippi when Jesus asks that question "Who do you say that I am?" And then panicking when Jesus tells him what "Messiah" means, about death, about rising again. And about Peter saying, "No, that cannot be so." And Jesus sternly rebuking him. Then, in the saddest story of all, Peter denying Jesus three times after he had told him he would die for him. Only, when the time came, the fear overwhelmed him. And the cock crowed. What does the crow of the cock do? It heralds the dawn, the coming of the light. The coming of Peter's realization who Jesus is and he, Peter, how flawed he is. Grey in character like the asphalt in the photo where the puddle is.

Yet how is it that Jesus shines light in our dark places? . . . Jesus says to Peter, in Matthew's Gospel, "You are Peter, and, on this rock, I will build my church." As if flaws are not a problem for Jesus. As if he knows that the Church will be built of ones such as Peter, ones such as us, too. As if puddles might reflect the glory of God.

Once a year, the Anglican schools come to our cathedral for a morning. The students go in groups to different parts of the cathedral, learning hymns and prayers for the worship that will conclude their time here. I have the best role, I think! I take my groups up to the gallery of the cathedral, to "the God View" one dean once called it, and there we look and we see in what ways the space speaks to us. Speaks to us of God. I

---

1 Michael Mayne, *Pray, Love, Remember* (London: Darton, Longman & Todd, 1999), p. 52.

tell them that our faith, put simply, says two things, really. Just two things. Two things are reflected into that grey puddle, in the spires of stone, with the golden autumn leaves around:

> God who made us, loves us and, when we make a mistake, God forgives us.

That's it really. It's there, writ large in Peter's story and it's there in our own. It's written in the story of individuals and communities, of nations and of the whole earth. And of humanity's relationship with the earth.

> God who made us, loves us and, when we make a mistake, God forgives us.

So, we look at the building from our God View in the gallery and we wonder about the different ways in which it speaks this truth. We think about the ways in which different people encounter truth, some through looking, some through listening, some through words, spoken and reflected upon, some in silence.

The space speaks through its very architecture, spires reaching to the heavens and the height of it; some of the students smile in wonder at the height of it, when they gaze from the gallery at the nave floor below. The space speaks almost of the "size" of God, the mystery of God, the "beyondness" of God. The space speaks through the windows and the reredos, telling the stories of the characters of our faith . . . Peter, of course, and angels, and bishops, and the crucifixion in all its horror in the window named "the love of God" window, and then images of our land in the clerestory windows above the nave. It is an incarnation we are talking about, in our cathedral. God is born in specific times and specific places. So, how wise of Cedar Prest to create images, in stained glass, of the God story set in our country, our culture.

The space speaks through the places for prayer and sacrament and music. The places where prayers have been said for the cathedral's over 150 years. The Lady Chapel where tears have been shed, as people prayed alone, and Eucharists have been celebrated every weekday morning for those who, sometimes bleary-eyed, have made the journey there at the start of day. The nave, where we have gathered in large numbers to welcome and farewell, to grieve and celebrate, to baptize, and wed, and at a funeral to commit a loved one's body, ashes to ashes, dust to dust, into the great love of God.

And the choir stalls, designed in memory of the chancels in monasteries and nunneries where almost hour by hour those devoted to the religious life sung antiphonally, across to one another. The choir stalls are home to the glorious music of our cathedral, singing the truth of God and the truth of living as the flawed created beings that we are.

Yes, as Michael Mayne said, "Although [we] use words with which to tell [our]story, it is invariably the space that speaks."

Jesus says to Peter, in Matthew's Gospel, "You are Peter and, on this rock, I will build my church" (Matthew 16:18). For flaws are not a problem for Jesus. As if he knows that the Church will be built of ones such as Peter, ones such as us, too.

As if in a grey puddle, on an early winter morning, we might see reflected the spires of a cathedral, our cathedral, this building that points to the most profound truth. Our cathedral, the very being of which is committed to speaking about the love of God whom we know in Jesus; the forgiveness of God spoken to Peter by the charcoal fire after the disciples caught fish for breakfast in the lake; the constant presence of God breathing life and healing into all creation.

CHAPTER 17

Blindness

She was standing in front of St Michael's Cathedral, arms outstretched, in the city where she lived, praying, it seemed, to Christ and the saints painted as a mural on the cathedral wall. An old lady. Her home, in the midst of being overrun, is Kyiv.

A newspaper picture showed a row of schoolchildren sitting like parcels on supermarket shelves, their faces covered in masks, for it is in the midst of pandemic that their homeland is being invaded. These children are preparing for a bombing raid in Druzhkivka.

In many cities and towns across Ukraine, buildings that, only days ago, housed families not unlike our own, human beings created and loved by God, are piles of rubble after the shelling that has taken place.

Ukraine has been invaded in a breaking of international law. Families known to loved ones across the world, including members of our own cathedral community, flee or hide or fight not knowing what violence the next day will bring.

As we gather in our cathedral this morning, our minds and hearts cannot but be affected by the struggles of our world. Two years into a pandemic, many years into living with deep concern about the health of our planet, we now find ourselves utterly shaken by these events that echo the Second World War.

So, we gather, we pray and we hear the singing of our choir. We look at one another in disbelief, and, then, we hear the words of scripture.

We may find ourselves struck by the image at the end of our Gospel reading of the house built without a foundation. When the river rose against it, it immediately fell in the force of the ensuing flood. We might feel as if that flood is rushing upon us, more particularly on the people of Ukraine. Images of scripture resonate. Which is exactly what God would have them do.

Through the voice of the prophet Isaiah, in this morning's reading from chapter 55, God speaks about scripture and how it reaches us. "My word that goes out from my mouth shall not return to me empty," God says, "but it shall accomplish that which I purpose and succeed in the thing for which I sent it" (Isaiah 55:11). We have an image of God speaking, and God's word reaching us, and God's word being heard, and responded to, and, somehow, in this, God's word returning to God.

We might reflect on this image as we find ourselves bystanders in the scene of Jesus' Sermon on the Plain. Jesus, in Luke's Gospel, is speaking with his disciples on a level place, the text says. After healing and freeing those who come to him for help, Jesus speaks, the word of God, we might think, to which Isaiah points us. In the words we heard read today, Jesus tells four parables, parables encouraging us to ponder our vocation as disciples. Parables that point to the struggle of it, really.

What do we do with Jesus' parables? What is he doing? His longing is that we hear, we know, we are transformed. He seems to understand us, that transformation as children of God is so difficult and happens rarely through instruction, direction. He might tell us what to do, where we fail, but we are unlikely to hear him, or if we do, we are unlikely to be changed by this. He knows that it is through our imaginations, our love of stories that he might reach us. If he can make us laugh, perhaps. Or leave us puzzled. Or in the case of the images with which this sermon began, leave us crying. "Tell the truth but tell it slant," the poet Emily Dickinson wrote. Jesus is often the expert in this.

So, he tells us parables. "Can a blind person guide a blind person? Will not both fall into a pit?" (Luke 6:39) he begins. One of the grounding passages of Luke's Gospel, which occurs in chapter 4, is Jesus' statement of his manifesto, if you like, his reading in the synagogue in Nazareth, a passage from Isaiah. He took up the scroll and, in the words he read, one phrase was of "recovery of sight to the blind".

Recovery of sight to the blind is one of his works, is part of his mission. It is small wonder he has the disciples, us, ponder the activity of the blind. It is small wonder that he would have us consider the possibility that we are blind, perhaps. He heals those who are physically blind, of course, but here he may be encouraging us to wonder about something different. It seems to be an aspect of life as a disciple to be a guide, a guide to others. An encourager, perhaps of those who journey with us in the life of faith, a welcomer to those who might tentatively walk through the doors of our cathedral for the first time. Fellow companions together at times when world events leave us utterly shattered.

"Can a blind person guide a blind person? Will not both fall into a pit?" he says.

We can smile at this. Of course, both may fall into a pit. We might wonder if we are not a little blind. We might allow ourselves to worry a little about what this means for our interactions with others.

The theme of blindness continues in the second parable:

> Why do you see the speck in your neighbour's eye, but do not notice the log in your own eye? (Luke 6:41)

Are we like this? Gazing on others, almost reassured by their faults. Failing to reflect on ourselves and our failings. Rarely wondering if we see clearly enough to judge another. Looking with judgement rather than compassion. What does Jesus mean when he tells us to take the logs out of our own eyes before we take the speck out of our neighbours' eyes? How can we take the log out of our eye if we cannot see?

We are trapped, you see, trapped by the parable. Which is just how Jesus would have us be. Ironically, it helps us see that we can't see. We cannot help ourselves, reflect on ourselves, let alone anyone else. And if we allow the muddle of this to stay for a little while . . . If we admit our tendency to see others' faults and rarely our own, if we sit with this . . . We might turn and look into the eyes of the one who tells the parable. We might look into the eyes of the one who sees us so clearly and longs to give us our sight. We might confess this to him. And he might wash our blind eyes and set us free.

Jesus then turns his attention to nature:

> No good tree bears bad fruit, nor again does a bad tree bear good fruit; for each tree is known by its own fruit. (Luke 6:43–4)

We may not be puzzled by these words, but Jesus quickly places them alongside us and our identity, which he says is found in our hearts. We might find ourselves quickly, worriedly, wondering: are our deeds good, are they evil? Is our heart good, is it evil? True, a good tree produces good fruit. Have we seen things this way? That our failures may be connected to the heart of us, our essence. That our good deeds may find their origin in our hearts. We are rarely all good or all evil, of course. Usually we are, again, a muddle of things. A little better some days than others. Sometimes regretfully flawed. Sometimes mercifully driven by the good. Jesus seems to want us to wonder about the heart of us, and only in sitting with him in his clear, loving, forgiving presence would we dare do this. Would we let him see our hearts, allow him to let us glimpse who we are.

Finally in the fourth parable we are given an image of a builder:

> Why do you call me "Lord, Lord", and do not do what I tell you? I will show you what someone is like who comes to me, hears my words, and acts on them. (Luke 6:46–7)

Before the parable we hear what Jesus longs for—that his disciples come to him, hear his words and act on them.

What does that look like . . . one who when building a house, digs a deep foundation upon a rock? This takes time, takes wisdom, takes care. What is the result of a builder building such a house? The spiritual writer John Shea puts it this way:

> Spiritual development entails hearing, understanding and acting. A question that would naturally arise for the disciples would be: if we hear, understand and act on what you say, what will we become? Jesus answers this question in a startling way. They will become flood proof. Raging rivers symbolize both the vicissitudes of life and the dark, sinister forces that seek to destroy human life. What Jesus offers is a foundation that can withstand

> those attacks. . . . Jesus the teacher wants disciples who can act and survive in a dangerous world.[1]

They will become flood proof. . . .

What does this mean, that we might be flood proof in the midst of the raging rivers that we see? How do we respond? How do we pray?

Jesus stands alongside us, as he stood in his human life, alongside those around him in all the struggles of human life, family life, community life, the life of his country. Stands alongside us even to dying at the hands of human violence. Perhaps this is how we pray. Standing alongside those suffering now in Ukraine and also, in many cases, those in Russia, protesting against this war.

Perhaps we let go of the endless news stories and the analysis of these events for a little while and we allow just one story to touch us. We allow ourselves to be vulnerable as those in the story are vulnerable. Perhaps we imagine ourselves praying in front of our cathedral, like the old woman in Kyiv. Perhaps we imagine ourselves a parent of one of the schoolchildren in Druzhkivka, sitting like parcels on a supermarket shelf. Perhaps we hear the story of one soldier who has died and we remember them. Perhaps that is what Jesus is saying. That we sit at the foot of his cross and pray, human beings caring about human beings, grieving as one can only grieve in a time of war, crying at the utter waste of it, the loss of it, the violence of it, longing that he might bring peace, begging him to heal the human blindness that brings about these things, knowing that, in the midst of this blindness, is our own.

---

1 John Shea, *The Relentless Widow* (Collegeville, MN: Liturgical Press, 2006), p. 55.

PART 5

Inspired by the poets

CHAPTER 18

Nothing can be loved at speed[1]

> In the time of King Herod, after Jesus was born in Bethlehem of Judea, wise men from the East came to Jerusalem, asking, "Where is the child who has been born king of the Jews? For we observed his star at its rising, and have come to pay him homage." (Matthew 2:1–2)

The thing about the wise men is that they looked. They gazed at the night sky, possibly for night after night, wondering about what they saw there. They kept watch, and they may have spent years keeping watch before they noticed that star. It was probably deeply woven into their way of being. A pattern of keeping watch and the faith of it. That one day there might be something new, a star that was different, a sign from God, that a new thing was about to take place.

The prophets told us to keep our eyes open. Isaiah spoke in this way, some of my favourite words of scripture:

> Do not remember the former things,
>   or consider the things of old.
> I am about to do a new thing;
>   now it springs forth, do you not perceive it?
> I will make a way in the wilderness
>   and rivers in the desert. (Isaiah 43:18–19)

"Do you not perceive it?" God said through the prophet. It's about a stance of keeping watch, of looking at the sky, and the events of the times,

---

[1] Michael Leunig, *The Prayer Tree* (Sydney: HarperCollins, 1990), pp. 32–3.

and the hearts of human beings. Being able to see God at work. God moving almost imperceptibly, God doing a new thing. That is always about making a way, bringing rivers to desert places, bringing life.

Looking at our world, we need the hope of this, don't we? Looking at a world where we struggle to see the possibility of peace, looking at a world engulfed in a pandemic, where we struggle to see the possibility of healing, looking at a world where the land and water and seas of our very home are under threat, we struggle to see the possibility of wholeness for creation.

Until we adopt a practice of gazing, gazing perhaps at the night sky, as the wise men did. For God's promise is that there will be a new thing. God's promise is that God will make a way in the wilderness, rivers in the desert. Only we didn't expect it to be seen in a star. And we didn't expect it in the vulnerability of a child.

Yes, they kept their eyes open, these wise men, and when the star shone in the night sky, they packed up their belongings and they sat upon their camels and they embarked on a long, long journey. Firstly, to Jerusalem to see the king, because they thought he would know. They asked him about the child.

> "Where is the child who has been born king of the Jews? For we observed his star at its rising, and have come to pay him homage." When King Herod heard this, he was frightened, and all Jerusalem with him; and calling together all the chief priests and scribes of the people, he inquired of them where the Messiah was to be born. They told him, "In Bethlehem of Judea . . . " (Matthew 2:2–5)

There was fear and there was threat. For the worldly king wasn't wise. He hadn't spent time watching the night sky, at all.

Would we embark on such a journey? Have we done so? Has a star risen in the darkness of our night sky . . . or has it shone in the words of a trusted friend . . . or in a growing sense of vocation, God sent, that took years to shine . . . or have words of scripture suddenly seemed to have been written just for us, that time, that day, as if God was trying to tell us something . . . or was it, as for Joseph, in a dream?

If God called to us, would we embark on such a journey? Cold, hard, frightening, away from all we know and all that comforts us, and yet, somehow, a journey that we just could not say no to? Would we pack up our belongings and climb on camels and go? Such journeys are not always about geography. They may be journeys in our souls. It may be about seeking forgiveness for something for which we have not been able to forgive ourselves. It may be about forgiving someone else. It may be about a gift that we know we have hidden in our souls and that we are too frightened to allow to shine. It may be about allowing ourselves to rest a little more, knowing that our worth lies not in what we do so much as who we are, made and loved in the hands of God. What might it be? There is a chance that we know. Or sometimes, the star that shines is utterly unexpected, and we were looking in quite a different direction, or perhaps we had forgotten what we knew as children, when the stars shine and call us to go on journeys on the backs of camels to stables in Bethlehem.

The journey was hard and needed to be taken slowly, carefully, with patience. But the star was there guiding them and the knowledge of the jealous king's threat warned them in a dream. It was given to help them know the preciousness and the vulnerability of the child, and the care they must take with the precious knowledge of his whereabouts when they found him. The journey needed great care. But the star was there, God was there, guiding them:

> There, ahead of them, went the star that they had seen at its rising, until it stopped over the place where the child was. When they saw that the star had stopped, they were overwhelmed with joy. On entering the house, they saw the child with Mary his mother; and they knelt down and paid him homage. Then, opening their treasure-chests, they offered him gifts of gold, frankincense, and myrrh. (Matthew 2:9–11)

The star was utterly dependable. We might remember that, when we find ourselves addressed by a star shining in the night sky and something in us tells us this is from God. It might be words of a friend, or words from scripture or a sense of vocation that takes years to emerge, to trust. The star can be trusted to lead us to the stable, to the one we are to worship, to our place of belonging, to the one who will heal us and save us, forgive us and bring us to life. To the one who will make a way in the wilderness and rivers in the desert. We can trust the star.

The three wise men worshipped when they saw . . . the baby wrapped in bands of cloth and lying in the manger, Mary, Joseph, the animals around . . . And, then, there were those three gifts.

It is interesting that in our passage from Isaiah this morning we heard of only two gifts:

> Arise, shine; for your light has come,
> and the glory of the LORD has risen upon you.
> For darkness shall cover the earth,
> and thick darkness the peoples;
> but the LORD will arise upon you,
> and his glory will appear over you.
> Nations shall come to your light,
> and kings to the brightness of your dawn . . .
> They shall bring gold and frankincense,
> and shall proclaim the praise of the LORD. (Isaiah 60:1–3,6)

As if the prophets might not have realized what lay ahead for the infant child. Gold for a king, frankincense for worship but then there is myrrh . . . myrrh for the anointing of his dead body. The kings must have sensed what lay ahead for the Christ child. Maybe their encounter with Herod helped them know. They could protect him now, by going home by another road, but the danger would catch up with the child in the end. And the three gifts tell Mary and Joseph what lies ahead.

They came with joy, remember, when they saw that the star had stopped, they were overwhelmed with joy. Might we be overwhelmed with joy? After our journey? The slow journey following our star, whatever it might be? Might we be overwhelmed with joy?

Opening our treasure chests, what shall we bring? All the years of keeping watch, all the effort of the long journey, and here, looking at the one we know we have come to be with, what shall we bring? Ourselves, I guess. The carol puts it, beautifully, we bring our hearts. The hearts that are restless until they are found in him, until they sit in the stable and know, that in this child is healing and forgiveness and meaning for each one of us, and each ordinary human being that we so love, our family and our friends, and all creation. We bring our hearts.

It is a slow thing, this vocation of the three kings, our vocation. Keeping watch for stars, travelling long journeys, and when our star stops, gazing and loving and being loved. It is a slow thing, this life as children of God, it needs our time.

Australian poet Michael Leunig knew that. He wrote about a journey and it might have been the journey to the stable in Bethlehem.

> Dear God,
> We pray for another way of being:
> another way of knowing.
> Across the difficult terrain of our existence
> we have attempted to build a highway
> and in so doing have lost our footpath.
> God lead us to our footpath:
> Lead us there where in simplicity
> we may move at the speed of natural creatures
> and feel the earth's love beneath our feet.
> Lead us there where step-by-step we may feel
> the movement of creation in our hearts.
> And lead us there where side-by-side
> we may feel the embrace of the common soul.
> Nothing can be loved at speed.
>
> God lead us to the slow path; to the joyous insights
> of the pilgrim; another way of knowing: another way of being.
> Amen.[2]

---

2 Leunig, *The Prayer Tree*, pp. 32–3.

CHAPTER 19

Awash with psalms

This weekend our city is awash with the psalms. A series of 12 concerts involving four different choirs entitled *150 Psalms* is being sung in our cathedral, in various churches, and in a synagogue. An exhibition of photographs housed in the Festival Centre has on display a photograph illustrating each psalm. Next Wednesday a seminar will take place in the cathedral where a Christian Hebrew scholar and a rabbi will reflect on the significance of the psalms in their respective traditions of faith.

So, this evening, at Choral Evensong, where week by week we reflect on one psalm as it is sung by our cathedral choir, I thought we would spend a little time exploring the significance of this moving and powerful set of texts in the life of faith.

The first and most important thing to note about the psalms is that they are to be articulated. To be spoken or sung. The second and just as important thing to notice is that they are an address, an address to someone, to a presence, to God. The writer and the speaker of the psalm is making an assumption, and that assumption is that the words *spoken* are *heard*. In fact, in many of the psalms, the one addressed also speaks their response. The psalms assume that we are not alone, and that the one who accompanies us is deeply concerned to hear whatever we have to say. There is no politeness in the psalms, no covering up the truth of joy or grief, fear or guilt. Whatever is being experienced can and, in fact, must be spoken.

Rowan Williams, former Archbishop of Canterbury, once described God as a presence that is a witness:

> The dependable presence that doesn't go away; the presence that remembers and holds in a single gaze what has been true and is

> true of us; the eternal, unshakeable witness to what we are. That presence is love. We are seen, known and held, but above all we are welcomed.[1]

What is particularly welcomed is our speech. For speech nurtures relationship and invites the possibility of transformation. Many of the psalms, in fact, tell a narrative of transformation.

The psalms articulate all the possibilities of human experience. They speak of joy in words of praise. They speak of trust in times of struggle. They speak of despair and the desperate need for rescue. They speak of the fury we experience when life is ripped away from us by violence or natural disaster or illness, and they speak of guilt, the awful guilt over what we have done, what we ought not to have done, and there is no health in us, as the prayer says.

David knew that guilt and from it he wrote the words of this evening's psalm, Psalm 51. David wrote them as he begged the forgiveness of God for a terrible sin. David coveted and took for himself Bathsheba, the wife of Uriah the Hittite and, in order to keep Bathsheba for himself, he arranged that Uriah be placed "in the forefront of the hardest fighting . . . so that he might be struck down and die" (2 Samuel 11:15). David broke the Ten Commandments, the law given by God to help the Israelite people live well with God and with one another. David committed a terrible sin:

> Have mercy upon me, O God, after thy great goodness
> according to the multitude of thy mercies
> do away mine offences. (Psalm 51:1)

In this first verse of the psalm, the two characters are clearly portrayed. God, to whom the psalm is addressed, is a God of mercy and goodness. The psalmist is the one who has caused offence, who in later verses describes himself as being a person of wickedness, sin and evil. The psalm is a plea for forgiveness. A plea spoken in the clear assumption

---

1 Rowan Williams, *Being Disciples* (London: SPCK, 2016), p. 32.

that the one who is addressed hears and will act. As the psalm goes on the restoration is imagined:

> Thou shalt purge me with hyssop, and I shall be clean
> thou shalt wash me, and I shall be whiter than snow.
> Thou shalt make me hear of joy and gladness
> that the bones which thou hast broken may rejoice.
> Turn thy face from my sins
> and put out all my misdeeds.
> Make me a clean heart, O God. (Psalm 51:7–10)

The psalmist then imagines a life in which, once reformed, he teaches others the ways and he lives a life of praise. The words that we sing each Sunday night as part of the *preces* are then sung to God:

> Thou shalt open my lips, O LORD
> and my mouth shall shew thy praise. (Psalm 51:15)

The psalm enacts the transformation and the relationship of the guilty one with their God is spoken in the psalm, so that forgiveness and restoration takes place.

In his book *The Spirituality of the Psalms*, Walter Brueggemann notes that human life seems to move through what might be thought of as *seasons*. He describes three seasons and identifies three different categories of psalms. "Human life consists in satisfied seasons of wellbeing that evoke gratitude for the constancy of blessing," he writes. Expression in such a season can be found in what Brueggemann names *psalms of orientation*. These psalms describe the "joy, delight, goodness, coherence, and reliability of God, God's creation, and God's governing law".[2]

Not all life, though, has the feel of a season of wellbeing. "Human life consists in anguished seasons of hurt, alienation, suffering and death.

---

[2] WalterBrueggemann, *The Spirituality of the Psalms* (Minneapolis: Ausgburg Fortress, 2002), p. 8.

These evoke rage, resentment, self-pity and hatred."[3] The psalms that befit these seasons of anguish Brueggemann calls *psalms of disorientation.*

Brueggemann describes the use of psalms of disorientation, one example of which is Psalm 22, "My God, my God, why have you forsaken me . . .", as an "*act of bold faith*. . . . because it insists that the world must be experienced as it really is and not in some pretended way. . . . it insists that all such experiences of disorder are a proper subject for discourse with God".[4] God invites us to speak the truth, and it is in speaking that truth that transformation might come.

Brueggemann describes a third season. A season which has at its heart the element of surprise. "Human life consists in turns of surprise," he writes, "when we are overwhelmed with new gifts from God, when joy breaks through despair".[5] The psalms that befit this season of surprise, of new light, where a human being might have thought they were forever to be in a place of darkness, are described as *psalms of new orientation.*

Psalms of disorientation such as this evening's psalm, Psalm 51, assume that all experience can be spoken to God and that God will hear and respond. In difficult times, though, it can be more comfortable to turn one's back on what is happening. Brueggemann writes, "The linguistic function of the psalms is that the psalm may *evoke reality* for someone who has engaged in self-deception and still imagines and pretends that life is well-ordered, when, in fact it is not." For example, a person guilty of a terrible sin, such as David, might deny their guilt or not even entertain the possibility of it. The psalm gives the guilty one words to speak to realize the reality of what they have done. Brueggemann goes on, "in such a case, *language leads experience*, so that the speaker speaks what is unknown and unexperienced until it is finally brought to speech. It is not this way until it is said to be this way."[6]

Language leads experience. The psalms lead us as we struggle to live well, whether we find ourselves in difficult times or in good. It is in

---

3 Brueggemann, *The Spirituality of the Psalms*, p. 8.

4 Brueggemann, *The Spirituality of the Psalms*, p. 27.

5 Brueggemann, *The Spirituality of the Psalms*, p. 8.

6 Brueggemann, *The Spirituality of the Psalms*, pp. 28–9.

speaking or singing the psalms that we are enabled to pray the truth in which we find ourselves and in praying that truth to be transformed in it.

Language leads experience. I wonder if the psalms might be the texts that lead us through the experience that is Lent. As we enter this time of reflection, this season when we might give a little extra time to pondering the presence of God, perhaps the psalms might be our guide. I certainly would not encourage us to attempt taking on the whole of the 150 Psalms as our city has done in photographs and music this Festival time, but perhaps one psalm might guide us. The morning psalm, Psalm 95, might be said each day in the dawn light, the evening psalm, Psalm 31, might be said as the day draws to a close; we might have a particular guilt that Psalm 51 will help us articulate or we might simply wish to spend Lent hearing God saying to us, words from Psalm 46, "Be still and know that I am God." A verse will do. It need not be even a whole psalm that guides us. A verse will do.

Our city is awash with the psalms this Festival time. May the words of the psalms nurture us as we embark on the holy Season of Lent.

CHAPTER 20

Love and fear

The Australian poet and cartoonist Michael Leunig wrote the following poem:

> There are only two feelings.
> Love and fear.
> There are only two languages.
> Love and fear.
> There are only two activities.
> Love and fear.
> There are only two motives,
> two procedures, two frameworks,
> two results.
> Love and fear.
> Love and fear.[1]

Jesus in a boat on the sea, in the story we heard read from Mark 4, seems to be saying something similar. It's like he is saying to the frightened disciples who are with him, "Love is with you, why are you afraid?"

It's at the end of the day, when evening has come, and Jesus says to some of the disciples, "Let us go across to the other side." To the other side of the sea, he means. So, leaving the crowd behind, they take him with them in the boat, just as he is, the text from Mark's Gospel says. "Just as he is"—what does that mean, we might wonder. Jesus has been teaching the crowd from a boat, teaching them in parables, the ones about the seeds. The parable of the sower, with its interpretation about the word, and the

[1] Michael Leunig, *A Common Prayer* (Sydney: HarperCollins, 1990), pp. 30–1.

parable of the mustard seed, of the kingdom of God being like a tiny seed. It's one of my favourite parables, because Jesus doesn't say the kingdom is like the great bush the seed grows into; he says the kingdom of God is like the tiny mustard seed. We might well imagine that this teaching has left them puzzled, worried even, as they embark on the journey in the boat to the other side of the sea, to Gentile territory.

A great gale arises, and the waves break over the boat, so that it is already being swamped. But Jesus is in the stern, asleep on the cushion; and they wake him up and say, "Teacher, do you not care that we are perishing?" He wakes up and rebukes the wind, and says to the sea, "Peace! Be still!" Then the wind ceases, and there is a dead calm. He says to them, "Why are you afraid? Have you still no faith?" (Mark 4:35–41).

Love is there, and fear. It is not difficult to imagine what they are afraid of. A great gale, waves in the boat. Many of the disciples are fishermen so it is not as if they don't understand the sea; but this is not a normal sea. This sea is life threatening. They are not exaggerating when they cry out to Jesus that they are perishing. There is another source of their fear, and that is his seeming lack of concern. "Teacher, do you not care?" they cry. When we are under threat, that we are alone in it, that no one cares and that no one can help, makes the situation all the worse. Their fear is of physical threat and of being alone in it.

Jesus, though, is not afraid. The storm at sea does not seem to frighten him. That he can sleep through it makes him all the more puzzling to them.

> There are only two motives,
> two procedures, two frameworks,
> two results.
> Love and fear.

Michael Leunig says. Jesus' framework is love. He seems to know himself so close to God whom he names "Abba"—a name that shows the trust that a little child has—that fear has no place, even in the midst of this storm at sea. His calming of the sea comes from *his calm*, his lack of fear. He seems to expect that the disciples will come to know a faith in him just like his faith in God. That the presence of love will overcome the presence of fear. And we might wonder about that.

The writer John Shea, reflecting on the disciples' response to the storm at sea, wrote the following:

> When we are in the midst of [dangers] our minds identify with what threatens us. They mirror the wind and the waves, making us as driven and tossed as we are. In this state we cannot receive from God. We cannot make the wisdom of Jesus's teachings work. However, Jesus's mind is not storm tossed. He sleeps . . . a picture of abiding peace in turbulence.[2]

For Jesus, love is his framework.

This morning's psalm, Psalm 133, speaks of a place where love might be the framework, to use Michael Leunig's words, where fear has no place. The psalm goes like this:

> Behold how good and how lovely it is:
>   when families live together in unity.
> It is fragrant as oil upon the head,
> . . . It is like a dew of Hermon:
>   like the dew that falls upon the hill of Zion.
> For there the LORD has commanded his blessing:
>   which is life for evermore.

It is good and lovely when families live together in unity, but we know that families are not always like this. In some families, fear and violence have taken the place of love, in fact may even be enacted in the name of love. A recent report, in the context of the Anglican Church, among many other reports on domestic violence, has revealed that scripture is at times used to justify family structures where violence and abuse take place in a home, or in a community.

---

[2] John Shea, *Eating with the Bridegroom* (Collegeville, MN: Liturgical Press, 2005), p. 156.

Two weeks ago, we pondered the idea of the sin against the Holy Spirit, a sin where a person would look on an act and, knowing it to be of God, would name it to be evil. Family or community structures, justified by scripture, where violence and abuse take place are signs of a different form of sin, but one we might think just as serious. There are two frameworks, love and fear, and fear has no place in family or a community grounded in the love of God, guided by the scriptures that are the word of God.

We might cry out as the disciples did in the storm; when there is violence and abuse, we might cry out wondering where God is, when God's word is being so misused. The theologian Jürgen Moltmann wrote a book on Jesus' crucifixion entitled *The Crucified God.* Where is God in the situation of violence and abuse, in homes and in other places? God is with the abused. God is in solidarity with the abused. Another theologian, James Alison, writes of Jesus having "the intelligence of the victim". He means that Jesus knows the victim's reality, stands in the midst of the victim's truth. Violence is never justified by God. Fear is never justified by love. Fear is never grounded in God.

Love is grounded in God.

When the storm rose at sea and the disciples were in the boat and Jesus was asleep, all they felt was fear. Fear for their safety. Fear that no one minded about whether they lived or died. Their minds "mirrored the wind and the waves", as John Shea said. We can, I think, understand them. The life of faith seems to move between love and fear, faith and fear.

We might glimpse something of the presence of God, one day, walking by the sea, perhaps, reading some words of insight from a writer in whom we have faith, knowing the loyalty of a friend when we are fed up with ourselves and we wonder if all who love us won't be fed up with us. We might glimpse the presence of God one day. We often think at those moments, "Ah, I get it now. God is with me. Love is with me. I need never be afraid again, whatever life holds. I'll remember this moment. The memory of it will sustain me, will help me trust in God."

Until we find ourselves again on a stormy sea and the struggle of being a faithful child of God returns. The dilemma of love and fear, faith and fear returns, with the longing to know God so close that we might be calm in the storm, trusting when we are at risk.

I guess what matters is that we do cry out to him. We do express our fear. We know that God cannot always calm the storms around us, the threats that living in a physical world brings. Perhaps what this story from Mark's Gospel is helping us to glimpse is that God reaches out always to calm the storm within us, always to speak, kindly, I suspect, to us saying, "Why are you afraid? Have you still no faith?" Always inviting us to know Jesus' mind that is not "storm tossed". His presence, so trusting in God's presence, that he can sleep even in the midst of a storm.

CHAPTER 21

At a time of exile

It is time for the voice of the prophets, in this Advent time. This time when the prophets' voices ring out, guiding us in the way of God, the way of waiting for God, of allowing the possibility of God. The prophets are not scientists. They do not speak truths honed in laboratories. They are not mathematicians, driven by those artists' ruthless logic. They are not writers of history, interviewing, sifting, analysing the stories of their time and place for patterns and motivations.

As an Old Testament scholar who loves the prophets, Walter Brueggemann says the prophets are poets. Poets who point to the truth of God, even, extraordinarily, bring about the action of God. Walter Brueggemann was reflecting on the beautiful words of the prophet Isaiah, written to the people of Israel in exile in Babylon, where all they knew, their place of worship, their king, their homes, were gone. Isaiah writes to God's shattered people in chapter 43 of his book:

> Do not remember the former things,
>   or consider the things of old.
> I am about to do a new thing;
>   now it springs forth, do you not perceive it?
> I will make a way in the wilderness
>   and rivers in the desert. (Isaiah 43:18–19)

Walter Brueggemann reflects:

> [The prophets] proclaim a new beginning with fresh actions from God that are wrought in this moment of exile, this crisis of dismantling.... these new actions of God that [the prophets]

> articulate are not new actions that are obvious on the face of it. . . . These prophets not only discerned the new actions of God that others did not discern, but they wrought the new actions of God by the power of their imagination, their tongues, their words. New poetic imagination evoked new realities in the community.[1]

Brueggemann, who describes his preacher as a poet, gives to that poet *extraordinary creative power*: "The poet in vivid imagination can create . . . "[2] he says. "It is a moment of utterance! . . . everything has now been changed by the poetic utterance, because the *poetry cannot be unsaid* . . . The word has been uttered and the juices of alternative possibility have begun to flow."[3]

We are in our own moment of exile, our own "crisis of dismantling", to use Brueggemann's words. The certainties, of which we in our most fortunate lives were barely conscious, are shaken, by a mutating virus, a changing climate and the consequences of our nations struggling to navigate a way through these things.

On this, the Third Sunday of Advent, we have the voice of the prophet Zephaniah to ponder:

> Sing aloud, O daughter Zion;
> shout, O Israel!
> Rejoice and exult with all your heart,
> O daughter Jerusalem!
> The Lord has taken away the judgements against you,
> he has turned away your enemies.
> The king of Israel, the Lord, is in your midst;
> you shall fear disaster no more.
> On that day it shall be said to Jerusalem:
> Do not fear, O Zion;

---

1 Walter Brueggemann, *Hopeful Imagination* (Philadelphia: Fortress Press, 1986), p. 2.

2 Walter Brueggemann, *The Word Militant: Preaching a Decentering Word* (Minneapolis: Fortress Press, 2010), p. 7.

3 Brueggemann, *The Word Militant*, p. 8.

> do not let your hands grow weak.
> The LORD, your God, is in your midst. (Zephaniah 3:14–17)

The Lord, your God, is in your midst. Zephaniah spoke these words to the people of God in exile and they ring out in our cathedral this day. Let us remember Brueggemann's words. "These prophets not only discerned the new actions of God that others did not discern, but they wrought the new actions of God by the power of their imagination, their tongues, their words. New poetic imagination evoked new realities in the community." The reality that is being evoked as we read and hear these words is the reality of God's presence among us.

The prophet poet then changes his address. The prophet steps back into the shadows and invites this God who is in our midst to speak.

What does God say? I . . .

> I will remove disaster from you,
> so that you will not bear reproach for it.
> I will deal with all your oppressors
> at that time.
> And I will save the lame
> and gather the outcast,
> and I will change their shame into praise
> and renown in all the earth.
> At that time I will bring you home,
> . . . says the LORD. (Zephaniah 3:18–20)

I will bring you home. Remember this is poetry we are hearing. The voice of God heard through the voice of the prophet poet.

This morning, we are also invited to hear the voice of a writer of letters. The Apostle Paul, writing to the people of Philippi, must have known the prophets' voice. He says in his letter:

> The Lord is near.

The Lord is near.

And he urges us in our response. The response that Zephaniah urges us in also.

The response imaged in the pink candle lit by our Cathedral Kids this morning.

Rejoice. The response of rejoicing.

Paul writes:

> Rejoice in the Lord always; again I will say, Rejoice. [Paul writes.] Let your gentleness be known to everyone. The Lord is near. Do not worry about anything, but in everything by prayer and supplication with thanksgiving let your requests be made known to God. And the peace of God, which surpasses all understanding, will guard your hearts and your minds in Christ Jesus. (Philippians 4:4–7)

The voice of the prophet tells us that God is in our midst. The voice of the letter writer urges the people to whom he writes to know that the Lord is near. Whilst we are not given certainty, we are not given proof, we are invited to allow these words to bring us to rejoicing.

We have heard the voice of the prophets; we have heard the voice of the letter writer. So, what of us, what of our voice? What shall our response be?

We have entered the Year of Luke's Gospel and so we hear of John the Baptist through the account of the writer of that Gospel.

John the Baptist speaks with a different tone; his voice urges repentance. A time of reflection on our lives, on those things of which we are ashamed, those patterns of being that we wish we could break. "You brood of vipers!" he calls those about him. Not exactly flattering, but they do listen. They do ponder his words. Then, they speak their own. What do they say? The crowds, the tax collectors, the soldiers, all speak up. All ask the same question.

"What should we do?" they ask.

"What should we do?"

What were the crowds and the tax collectors and the soldiers to do?

To the crowd John the Baptist says, "Whoever has two coats must share with anyone who has none; and whoever has food must do likewise." To the tax collectors he says, "Collect no more than the amount prescribed for you." To the soldiers, he says, "Do not extort money from anyone by threats or false accusation, and be satisfied with your wages."

They are to respond to those with whom they come into contact with generosity and justice. Generosity and justice.

Which reminds us of the voice of another of the prophets, the prophet Micah:

> What does the LORD require of you,
> [Micah asked those who were listening to him],
> but to do justice, and to love kindness,
> and to walk humbly with your God? (Micah 6:8)

As we gather in our cathedral on this Third Sunday of Advent, what should we do?

> Do justice, and to love kindness,
> and to walk humbly with your God.

Knowing that this God is in our midst, rejoicing that our God is in our midst.

CHAPTER 22

Remembering of war

What passing-bells for these who die as cattle?
    —Only the monstrous anger of the guns
    Only the stuttering rifles' rapid rattle
Can patter out their hasty orisons.
No mockeries now for them; no prayers nor bells;
    Nor any voice of mourning save the choirs,—
The shrill, demented choirs of wailing shells;
    And bugles calling for them from sad shires.

What candles may be held to speed them all?
    Not in the hands of boys, but in their eyes
Shall shine the holy glimmers of goodbyes.
    The pallor of girls' brows shall be their pall;
Their flowers the tenderness of patient minds,
And each slow dusk a drawing-down of blinds.

Wilfred Edward Salter Owen was an English poet and soldier. His war poetry on the horrors of trenches and gas warfare stood in contrast to the public perception of war at the time and to the confidently patriotic verse written by earlier war poets such as Rupert Brooke. One of his best-known poems is this poem entitled "Anthem for Doomed Youth". Wilfred Owen was killed in action on 4 November 1918, a week before the war's end, at the age of 25. He chose poetry to write of the truth and lies of war. Poetry, photographs, tears, nurture our remembering of war . . .

The remembering of the First World War is also nurtured by a particular flower, the poppy. Poppies produce seeds that can lie dormant in the soil for as long as one hundred years. The seeds need light to grow so they only germinate in disturbed soils. The digging of trenches, the bombs and the mass cemeteries that decimated Europe's landscape during World War I brought about the blooming of millions of poppies on the disrupted soil.

And so they are the symbol of remembrance for us, of remembering the lives of those who fell on that soil, of remembering the grief of those who loved them, of remembering the horror and waste of war. Poppies, photographs, tears and poetry nurture our remembrance of war, nurturing our longing for forgiveness for it, nurturing our guilt, our grief that the wars just keep on, that our need for power, our insecurity and fear, means that the wars just keep on being fought.

Poppies, photographs, tears and poetry, nurture our remembering of war . . .

It might be easy to rage and wonder and believe we would never have a part in it. To watch Ukraine in our time and place from afar, and wonder how it could be that in the midst of a climate crisis, in the midst of famine, in the midst of a pandemic, we could watch the brutal destruction of the homeland of one by another. We could believe we would never have a part in it. We might be careful about that. I grew up watching a historian write his great book on the First World War inspired by the words that informed the title of his book. The words were these:

> A man might rage against war; but war from among its myriad faces, could always turn towards him one, which was his own.[1]

Our faces, our hearts, our thoughts, our beings are not immune from what it is that makes for war.

> . . . war from among its myriad faces, could always turn towards us one, which was our own . . .

Jesus knew that, knew our hearts, knows our hearts. Jesus knows that each one of us might be drawn into sin that we could not have imagined.

---

1 F. E. Manning quoted in preface of Trevor Wilson, *The Myriad Faces of War* (Cambridge: Polity Press, 1986).

He knows that our longing for security, our fear, might clutch at us in such a way that violence, that war is possible.

Jesus knows us. And so, he tells us a parable:

> Look at the fig tree and all the trees; as soon as they sprout leaves you can see for yourselves and know that summer is already near. So also, when you see these things taking place, you know that the kingdom of God is near. . . . be on your guard . . . (Luke 21:29–30,34)

His whole message is this really: look! Look around you at what the trees are doing and you will know what the seasons are doing. Look around you at what is happening in the world and you will know what human hearts are doing. Look at your own heart, be on your guard, keep awake. Look for what is in you and for what is in the hearts of others. Look also for the signs of God, for the sprouting of leaves in the fig trees. Look for signs of God, signs of the kingdom of God. Look, ponder, remember . . .

As we gather at this Evensong service dedicated to a time of remembrance for those who died in war, let us look, look at the world far from us and near to us, for signs of human sin and frailty, for signs of God's redemption. Look and pray. Ponder the reality of war in our time and place.

What flowers will grow in the soil of Ukraine when the war ends? What flowers will grow in the soil dug up by bombs and tears, bullets and blood? Will they be sunflowers? The Poet Laureate Simon Armitage crafted a poem in solidarity with the people of Ukraine. He thought there would be sunflowers, the national flower of Ukraine. He named his poem "Resistance".

> It's war again: a family
> carries its family out of a pranged house
> under a burning thatch.
>
> The next scene smacks
> of archive newsreel: platforms and trains
> (never again, never again),

toddlers passed
over heads and shoulders, lifetimes stowed
in luggage racks.

It's war again: unmistakable smoke
on the near horizon mistaken
for thick fog. Fingers crossed.

An old blue tractor
tows an armoured tank
into no-man's land.

It's the ceasefire hour: godspeed the columns
of winter coats and fur-lined hoods,
the high-wire walk

over buckled bridges
managing cases and bags,
balancing west and east—godspeed.

It's war again: the woman in black
gives sunflower seeds to the soldier, insists
his marrow will nourish

the national flower. In dreams
let bullets be birds, let cluster bombs
burst into flocks.

False news is news
with the pity
edited out. It's war again:

> an air-raid siren can't fully mute
> the cathedral bells—
> let's call that hope.[2]

Will it be sunflowers that are gathered, when the war ends, when the remembering begins? Cut in bunches, placed in vases on mantelpieces and altars, clung to before they are scattered on graves? Will it be sunflowers that inspire remembrance in Ukraine?

As, when that war finally ends, we cry to God, surely never again, never again.

The poppies and the sunflowers remind us of all the dear souls who were lost in war, remind us of the lives of those who fell on that soil in which the flowers grow, remind us of the grief of those who loved them, help us ponder again the horror and waste of war.

And hear the words of the poem again, that even in the midst of war,

> an air-raid siren can't fully mute
> the cathedral bells—

And wonder if we too might call that hope.

---

2 Simon Armitage, used with permission.

CHAPTER 23

The spirituality of a cathedral—the nave

Love bade me welcome: yet my soul drew back,
    Guilty of dust and sin.
But quick-eyed Love, observing me grow slack
    From my first entrance in,
Drew nearer to me, sweetly questioning
    If I lacked anything.

"A guest," I answered, "worthy to be here":
    Love said, "You shall be he."
"I, the unkind, ungrateful? Ah, my dear,
    I cannot look on thee."
Love took my hand, and smiling did reply,
    "Who made the eyes but I?"

"Truth, Lord; but I have marred them; let my shame
    Go where it doth deserve."
"And know you not," says Love, "who bore the blame?"
    "My dear, then I will serve."
"You must sit down," says Love, "and taste my meat."
    So I did sit and eat.

"Love bade me welcome"—this poem by George Herbert that invites us to ponder a spirituality of our cathedral.

This year we are focusing on many different aspects of this building that is, and has been, precious for so many over 150 years. For four evenings, we will ponder the spirituality of this place, focusing on four different aspects: the nave, the choir, the altar, and the flags. Four sermons cannot begin to exhaust the depth of this our cathedral building, but I hope at least to begin our reflections.

The idea for this series comes from a book written by a former Dean of Westminster Abbey, Michael Mayne, entitled *Pray, Love, Remember*. In this book, written for Lent, Michael Mayne devotes each of his chapters to a place in the Abbey, reflecting on its particular meaning for him, remembering some of the key events that took place there and including excerpts from his diaries. Many of the other ideas for this series of sermons will come from parishioners, particularly Rosie Hamilton and other tour leaders who through my time here have generously given their own particular insights into what inspires them about the cathedral. I am particularly indebted to Canon Bill Goodes who wrote a "Spirituality Tour of the Cathedral" to help me with these sermons.

Love bade me welcome. Bade us welcome, really.

We enter the cathedral through an open door, and we enter it from the world. One wonderful aspect of our cathedral is its almost always open door. Blessed by welcomers who give generously of their time and seem so often to delight graciously in meeting strangers from across the globe, the building, the spires of which reach to the sky, lifting our eyes and hearts from the streets and the daily concerns of our lives, invites us in. Surrounding our cathedral are signs of so many aspects of the world from which we come, a busy street, an oval, a garden with a cross of sacrifice, offices, hospitals, cafes and shops, places devoted to education, religious and otherwise, bus stops with children waiting, not always patiently, for the journey home.

The incarnation is about God being with us in a particular time and place, God alongside us wherever we are, whatever our circumstances, God forgiving our failures, leading us through times of struggle.

As we enter the cathedral, the nave opens out before us. William Butterfield, who made the original design for the cathedral, a design which Edward Woods took over and modified, planned a single large space that would embrace all worshippers, each with their own part to play. The word *nave* comes from the Latin word for ship. The building helps us see ourselves embarking on a journey surely, for those who designed and crafted and now care for this building, a journey of faith in God who we know in Christ. Our lives of faith begin, traditionally, with the sacrament of baptism and so it is fitting that the font, where baptism takes place, is just inside the West Door. The nave seems to invite us to sit and take part as we so often do week by week at services and sometimes at concerts, but the nave also invites us to move along this journey. The aisle is a place of movement, and the end of our journey is seen if we lift up our eyes. Christ in Glory is portrayed on the reredos, one of the many visual guides to our story of faith which rises beautifully up above the high altar. This image may or may not speak to us of heaven, the great mystery of our home in death. What matters is that our faith speaks of death not as a defeat, an extinguishing, but as a part of human and created life that is inhabited by God. Death has been inhabited and defeated by Jesus. All our life and our death is embraced by this faith and the nave of our cathedral is an image of this truth.

The open door and the nave invite us into a story. Michael Mayne reflects on this:

> The Church's chief task is to be the living reminder in every age of the divine story, a reminder in its annual recounting of the stories of Christmas, Holy Week, Easter and Pentecost, names which describe how the Christ-like God has acted within the confines of history. Actions which are definitive for all future time but which are spelled out in the homely language of one man's life and teaching and healing, and loving and forgiving, and suffering and dying. Our task is to make connections between his story and ours, between our little lives and the great life of God within us, but also (for example, and more remarkably) between our sufferings and God's suffering in Jesus Christ. For not only is that connection one of the central truths on which Christian belief rests, it is also the most comforting and affirming reality, and the starting point to turn whatever suffering we may have to face to creative ends.[1]

We are invited into a story, God's story. This story is told in word and sacrament, in music, glass, wood and stone. The key image of this story

---

1 Michael Mayne, *Pray, Love, Remember* (London: Darton, Longman & Todd, 1999), pp. 76–7.

is the cross, Jesus' cross; this cathedral is in the shape of a cross. During Choral Evensong through Lent, the story of Jesus' passion is told, reminding us of the centrality of this story as we prepare for Holy Week during the precious piece of time that is Lent.

We will spend time on the telling of the story of Jesus next week when we reflect on the choir of this cathedral, the place where the music is sung, the organ played. The gathered community is held in the nave whilst these storytellings spread out before us; the nave is the place where we ponder and pray, where we sit and hear, where we reach out to one another with open hands, saying each time we gather for Holy Communion, "Peace be with you."

"Peace be with you." The words in which we affirm, what God surely knows and hopes we will know, the value of each person seated around us. Friend and stranger, those whose lives and struggles we hold dear and those we have never met, those, perhaps, who have caused us pain and who we long to forgive. God's peace is offered to one another in the heart of the nave. Our gathering together in the nave and the peace we offer one another reminds us that we must, in Michael Mayne's words about his Abbey, "witness to the truth that every single human being, even the brassiest, gum-chewing, T-shirted, travel-weary tourist, stands each in the splendour of its own existence and is of unique worth in the sight of God".[2] Our Dean often reminds us that our cathedral's ministry is threefold—for our own community, for the diocese for whom we are "mother church" and for the city. Our welcoming and gathering in the nave reminds us of the truth that each of these ministries is of utter value to God.

The primary purpose for which we gather is worship. Michael Mayne writes that "those who built our churches created spaces intended to arouse in those who entered them a sense of entering a special space, evoking a sense of awe which is the beginning of worship. A space in which the offering of the *Opus Dei* [the daily work of God], day in, day out, year in, year out, for centuries has created a kind of holy rhythm that has invaded the very stones."[3] Perhaps not quite centuries for our

---

2 Mayne, *Pray, Love, Remember*, p. 8.

3 Mayne, *Pray, Love, Remember*, p. 19.

cathedral in its 150th anniversary, but we know what he means—and we commit ourselves to the centuries ahead.

Each weekday at 7.30 a.m., we embrace this holy rhythm as we celebrate the Eucharist in the Lady Chapel, the small communities that have gathered often joining one another for breakfast in one of the cafes nearby after the service. Each weekday at 8.45 a.m. we say Morning Prayer, remembering day by day each month the names of all who are on our cathedral roll. Each Wednesday at 5.30 p.m. we sing Choral Evensong, praying for parishes in our diocese and lighting candles for peace in the world . . . and then there is Sunday. The Eucharist is celebrated twice on Sunday morning and Evensong is sung on Sunday night. In the nave are gathered regular members of our congregation and visitors, those who wish to become involved and build friendships, and those who wish to be left in peace to drink in the worship alone.

Our cathedral doors open to gather in and welcome all who enter the nave with a sense that what they have entered is the house of God, the great love of God, the story of God. Then the doors open to send us out. Blessed by this love, we might go into the world to share that love perhaps, to speak of the story of God who we know in Christ, to encourage one another to offer welcome to strangers, to give generously to those in need. Blessed by this love to see the world a little more as God sees it, loved, blessed, broken, oh so loved. As George Herbert said,

> Love bade me welcome: yet my soul drew back,
>   Guilty of dust and sin.
> But quick-eyed Love, observing me grow slack
>   From my first entrance in,
> Drew nearer to me, sweetly questioning
>   If I lacked anything.

Next week we'll ponder our souls drawing back, guilty of dust and sin. As we reflect on what we call the choir, the place where music is sung and played, the place where the psalms are chanted, the place where the love and forgiveness of God is known in ways that our minds cannot quite understand.

CHAPTER 24

The spirituality of a cathedral—the choir

Last Sunday, in the first of our Evensong sermon series looking at the spirituality of our cathedral in this year of its 150th anniversary, we pondered the nave—we found there a place of welcome and also a place of journey, we found there a place where our value in God's eyes is affirmed and a place where we offer to one another God's peace. We found there an open door that sends us out into the world to share God's love in generosity.

This sermon series is woven with George Herbert's poem "Love Bade Me Welcome", and we closed last week's sermon with the first verse; tonight, we will begin also with the second:

> Love bade me welcome: yet my soul drew back,
>   Guilty of dust and sin.
> But quick-eyed Love, observing me grow slack
>   From my first entrance in,
> Drew nearer to me, sweetly questioning
>   If I lacked anything.
>
> "A guest," I answered, "worthy to be here":
>   Love said, "You shall be he."
> "I, the unkind, ungrateful? Ah, my dear,
>   I cannot look on thee."
> Love took my hand, and smiling did reply,
>   "Who made the eyes but I?"

God welcomes us and forgives us, God longs to give us life in places of fear and illness and death. This is at the heart of the Christian story . . .

but we do draw back. For we are so very aware of the guilt that mars us. We are indeed guilty of dust and sin, we may know this well. Or it may be an unease, a doubt, a fear, that causes this hesitation. But "quick-eyed love", indeed, draws nearer.

This drawing back can at times be as a result of a numbness, a shock. All who have witnessed or heard of the shooting in Christchurch, New Zealand, in recent days will know this shock, will know horror, will know a sense of helplessness in the face of ruthless violence, will be left wondering about a world at once so beautiful and yet so cruel. How might it be that the "quick-eyed love" of God draws near to those gathered in cathedrals and churches and mosques and halls across the world, when such grief is at hand?

In this, the second sermon in our Evensong series about the spirituality of our cathedral, we will explore ways in which God, described by George Herbert as "quick-eyed Love", draws nearer, in which our "God-made eyes" might look upon God in this place. This evening we will reflect on the choir, the place in the cathedral where the choir sings, where the organ is played and where the scriptures are read, and we will ponder the way in which God reaches out to us, not only in word and music but also in glass and wood and stone.

This evening and each evening in these first four weeks of Lent the choir has sung as our introit *Locus Iste* by Anton Bruckner. The choir have sung this piece in many places; it is their "party piece". I have heard them sing it on a hill overlooking Salisbury Cathedral, and in the Catacombs in Rome. Wherever they travel they sing it, but tonight they sang it in their home, "the choir". This evening in the second of this series, we will spend time pondering the choir. By this we mean not our beloved and greatly talented group of cathedral singers but the space in which they sing.

For the choir is the place in the cathedral where the ministry of music takes place. And, perhaps, when our souls draw back, in guilt or in shock and grief, when we hesitate in response to Love's welcome, one way that God reaches out to us, draws nearer to us, is through music. The music of our cathedral is based on cathedral music across the world and especially in England where the monastic tradition is followed—as we see in our choir—with monks sitting opposite one another, chanting psalms and canticles in alternate verses from one side to another. The music of the choir is upheld and enhanced by the music of the organ; the console and pipes rise up above the place of the choir. One of the great celebrations in this cathedral at this time is the restoration of the organ that has taken place over the past two years. With its shining new casework, the organ is a symbol in music of the blessing that ensues when a community of people gather together to support a project dear to their heart.

When we allow ourselves to be touched by music we approach it with humility, with vulnerability, we allow it to reach us, possibly even to transform us; we allow music to open our eyes to the beauty and the struggle of life, to the possibility of God and love and redemption.

One contemporary composer said the following about the place of music in the struggle of faith:

> Consciously I am certainly an atheist, but I do not say it out loud because if I look at Bach I cannot be an atheist. Then I have to accept the way he believed. His music never stops praying. How can I get closer if I look at him from the outside? I do not believe in the Gospels in a literal fashion, but a Bach fugue has the crucifixion in it—as the nails are being driven in. In music I am always looking for the hammering of the nails. . . . that is a dual vision. My brain rejects it all. But my brain isn't worth much.[1]

When our souls draw back, music prays for us, it seems.

God reaches us in other ways in a cathedral. The building itself is a work of art. Its towers reaching for the heavens, its high roof, the long view which can be seen so well from the gallery all impress on us that, to quote a chorister who once spoke to me about faith, "When I come into the cathedral I know there is something bigger than me and my problems." Or, as Michael Mayne, former Dean of Westminster Abbey, wrote in *Pray, Love, Remember*, the book from which the idea for this sermon series came:

---

1 John Eliot Gardiner in his book on Bach, *Bach, Music the Castle of Heaven*, quoted this statement from the contemporary György Kurtág.

> I never fail to be moved by how affected [visitors] are by the atmosphere in this historic, holy and storied space. Although I use words with which to tell its story, it is invariably the space that speaks.[2]

It is the space that speaks of God.

Returning to the choir, we find ourselves drawn in different ways into the story of God. At one end of the choir, where the long line of the building meets the second of the transepts which cross at right angles, above it we see the Lantern, symbol of light overcoming darkness, imagery for Jesus found particularly in the Gospel of John. Below the lantern we find the *cathedra*, from which the cathedral gets its name. It is the bishop's seat of teaching, the one who is responsible for upholding the faith of the Church.

Situated at the other end of the choir, within easy view of the congregation, we find a lectern, literally a place where words are read. Our lectern is in the shape of an eagle, the bird who would carry the word of God to the whole world. The story of God, read from Old Testament and the New, is heard day by day, Sunday by Sunday. Sermons are preached from it, prayers and hymns based on it, psalms sung from it. The cathedral's vocation is to help those who enter its doors to know that their story belongs in the great story of God, told in scripture.

The stone building is woven with other forms of art, art which tells God's story in ways other than words. The stained-glass windows, placed in every wall of the cathedral, speak of our story of faith and the characters of our faith. As we enter the nave, we see in the lower windows kings and queens, missionaries, monks and bishops. If we lift our eyes, we see the clerestory windows created by Cedar Prest. Struck by a cathedral that seemed so deeply connected to England and to have little connection with the land on which it was built, she designed a set of windows using the image of the vine from John 15, that connect the images of the Australian landscape with images from scripture. Glass, again, imaging our story woven into God's story. The windows of our

---

2 Michael Mayne, *Pray, Love, Remember* (London: Darton, Longman & Todd, 1999), p. 52.

cathedral span in style the full 150 years of the building's history, the most modern being the Magdalene window above the St Barnabas door, a window that portrays a resurrection scene which celebrates the ministry of women.

In a cathedral dedicated to St Peter, we find many references to our flawed and utterly human saint. Perhaps my favourite windows are in the Lady Chapel, one group of which represent one of the most poignant of all the Gospel stories. The scene is set by a charcoal fire. Jesus, risen from the dead, is questioning Peter three times about his love for him, forgiving three times the denials that so tore them both apart at the time of Jesus' trial. The weaving of Jesus' words into the windows help those gazing at them to enter powerfully into the scene. Love is bidding us welcome again. Our souls, like Peter's, drawing back, only to have love reaching out again with forgiveness.

Glass is not the only visual medium for the telling of God's story and the nurturing of our prayers. The beautifully carved oak reredos above the High Altar portrays Christ in Glory surrounded by angels and characters of our faith, as well as showing four scenes from our patron saint's life of faith.

"Love bade me welcome." In our cathedral we find ourselves made welcome in so many ways. This evening we have begun our reflections in the choir remembering that God reaches out to us in music, music which also helps us offer our prayers in reply to God. Music prays, remember. God invites us in as we gaze on lovingly crafted wood and glass and stone. God reaches out to us in the words of scripture, scripture that tells the story of God, inviting us into the story that is our home.

Tonight we sit in our cathedral conscious of the fact that the human heart is capable of great hatred as well as great love. We know that when that great hatred overpowers a person, unimaginable violence and suffering can take place. Then, strangely, mercifully, we witness responses of great love and solidarity and compassion. How might a cathedral enfold us as we struggle to sit with such truths? Our story is of one who knew these truths, embraced these truths for us, that we might know that even in the darkest of human experiences we are not alone. Through God's embrace in Jesus of hatred, love will never be extinguished, never be overcome. Perhaps in the end what a cathedral gives us is itself. And that, as Michael Mayne, former Dean of Westminster Abbey wrote, it is the space that speaks. Perhaps when suffering is so very great, it is the building and the silence that holds us in God's precious welcome.

CHAPTER 25

The spirituality of a cathedral—the altar

Two Sundays ago, in the first of our Evensong sermon series looking at the spirituality of our cathedral in this year of its 150th anniversary, we pondered the nave—we found there a place of welcome and also a place of journey; we found there a place where our value in God's eyes is affirmed, and a place where we offer to one another God's peace; we found there an open door that sends us out into the world to share God's love in generosity.

Last Sunday we spent time exploring the spirituality of the choir, the place where our cathedral choir sings and our newly restored organ is played, the place where the scriptures are read from the lectern in the form of an eagle, and from where we can gaze in all directions at God's story made visible in glass and wood and stone.

This sermon series is woven with George Herbert's poem "Love Bade Me Welcome", and its final verse speaks to the place of our reflection this evening. God, described as "quick-eyed love", has pointed out to the one speaking the poem that love made the poet's eyes. The poet responds:

> "Truth, Lord; but I have marred them; let my shame
>   Go where it doth deserve."
> "And know you not," says Love, "who bore the blame?"
>   "My dear, then I will serve."
> "You must sit down," says Love, "and taste my meat."
>   So I did sit and eat.

Love invites us, flawed but forgiven, to a banquet.

Tonight, in the third of our series, we will spend time at the altar and the sacraments that take place there. Only there is more than one altar here in St Peter's Cathedral. Altars where we gather to remember Jesus breaking the bread and offering the cup of wine at his last supper with his disciples, the night before his passion and death. Altars are about Eucharist, remembering.

Our different altars give insight into different theologies, really, different ways of understanding God. The High Altar, situated at the end of the cathedral, speaks of a God who is transcendent, distant, always beyond our reach. The Book of Common Prayer Communion is celebrated here each Sunday at 8 a.m. Above the High Altar stands the beautifully carved oak reredos which portrays Christ in Glory, surrounded by angels and characters of our faith, as well as showing four scenes from our patron saint Peter's life of faith. The High Altar is adorned with the lovely needlework of the altar frontals—yet another art form that nurtures our prayers—and what a privilege it is to witness the highly skilled needleworkers at work, on Monday mornings, once a month, as they restore and create the linen and needlework for our worship. You will notice this evening that the altar frontal has turned from Lenten purple to white, as we prepare to remember the feast day of the Blessed Virgin Mary.

The liturgical year follows the story of Jesus from the awaiting of his birth and the coming of the kingdom from Advent, through Christmas, Epiphany, Lent, Holy Week, Easter and Pentecost. As the story unfolds, the different liturgical colours give witness to the different moods and ways of prayer of each of the seasons. Purple for reflective times, white for celebration, red for the Holy Spirit and for remembering those who died a martyr's death, and green . . . green for what I call the precious ordinary days.

The nave altar gives a different insight into God. We gather at 10.30 a.m. each Sunday morning around this altar, opening our hands, reaching out in vulnerability and need for God, and as we do so we give witness to a God who is with us, in our midst, God who is to be found where we are, at the heart of our lives with all their blessings and struggles.

The third altar at which Holy Communion is celebrated is in the Lady Chapel. This chapel dedicated to Our Lady, Mary the Mother of Jesus, points to her presence in several ways. Three lilies, the traditional symbol of Mary, decorate the centre of the silver altar cross, lilies are embroidered into the kneelers around the altar and a portrayal of Mary by Voitre Marek is on the wall.

The Eucharist is celebrated in this chapel each weekday at 7.30 a.m. Small congregations of people gather to reach out for God's blessing in bread and wine before they go out into the world to embrace whatever their day holds. Small funerals, baptisms, weddings, take place there. This intimate space lends itself to quiet prayer and visitors often spend time in this chapel reflecting on whatever is on their hearts, that time, that day. Occasionally, a prayer for healing and an anointing with holy oil is shared in this gentle place dedicated to Mary; once in a while a confession is made and the words of absolution are spoken there by a priest.

Each time a Eucharist is celebrated the words of confession and absolution are spoken. Michael Mayne, former Dean of Westminster Abbey, wrote in *Pray, Love, Remember*, the book from which the idea for this sermon series came, about confession:

> Sin is our refusal to become who we truly are. In those moments when I kneel before God in penitence, or join with others in confession, sometimes I am aware of specific faults: unloving words, thoughtless conduct, selfish actions. I am aware of not caring enough. But chiefly I am aware of a much more subtle temptation: to settle for less than I might be. To choose the lesser good. To lack curiosity and wonder. . . . Not to perceive that I am 'fearfully and wonderfully made' in God's image. And when I ask God to forgive me, I do so, because in settling for less than I am created to be, I know not what I do.[1]

We often speak of turning away from our sins, but I think we turn towards them first. Look at them, remember them, feel the discomfort of them, before we speak to God in confession and hear the words of forgiveness, the words that remind us that God knows us as we are, forgives us as we are, setting us free to try again in our vocation of living as God created us to live.

---

1 Michael Mayne, *Pray, Love, Remember* (London: Darton, Longman & Todd, 1999), p. 46.

The cathedral is at its heart a place to pray. What are we doing when we pray, we might wonder? Michael Mayne writes:

> Prayer is not an escape from life, a few minutes cut out from life, but a regular disciplined reminder that all life is lived in God's presence, a marvelling at God's love shown in Christ, a thankful responding to that transcendent reality by whom we are held in being. Prayer, then, is not primarily something I do in order to achieve something, but something I do because this is the sort of creature I am called to be: one who has an intuitive sense of the transcendent, one who has a muffled but persistent sense of the presence of the holy.[2]

The Jesuit book that we are using in this cathedral for our Lenten studies this year quotes another writer describing prayer as "taking a long loving look at the real".[3] Strangers and members of our community gather in this cathedral around the altars at services of Holy Communion, or quietly alone in the nave or the Lady Chapel to take a "long loving look" at what is real in their lives, in the lives of those they love and in the lives of strangers whose stories have touched their hearts in the news. This "long loving look" is taken surrounded by the truth that Jesus' Spirit is with us, guiding our prayers.

In each of our reflections on the spirituality of different places in our cathedral we have found not only wood and glass and stone, not only word and sacrament but also . . . us. The people of God . . . In the nave we found the welcomers and stewards and tour guides essential to nurturing God's welcome in the cathedral. In the choir it was, of course, the musicians. When we ponder the altars in our cathedral and the liturgies, the works of the people, that take place there, it is the liturgy team that is essential.

When I first came to be a priest in this cathedral, I was overawed. It was the liturgy team particularly that put me at my ease. Their home is

---

2 Mayne, *Pray, Love, Remember*, p. 24.

3 Walter Burghardt, quoted in James Martin, SJ, *The Jesuit Guide to (Almost) Everything: A Spirituality for Real Life* (New York: HarperOne, 2012), p. 8.

the sacristy—and the servers' vestry—the places where the robes and vessels are stored, where liturgy is prepared. This team of MCs (Masters of Ceremonies) and servers, vergers and acolytes, holds the liturgy together and is responsible for it. The priests play their part, but the liturgy team carry us. They hold onto the sacred knowledge that is at the heart of cathedral worship, and it is clear that they hold it sacred, handing it down to each fledgling server, each new verger or MC. The liturgy team is a place of welcome, gathering in students who come to Adelaide from overseas, children whose parents bring their families here to worship.

The final place in our cathedral on which we will reflect this evening is the aumbry. Behind the two small wooden doors on the left-hand side of the High Altar we find a cupboard in which is placed the reserved sacrament, the consecrated bread and wine, reserved from Eucharists that have taken place at one of the three cathedral altars. The red light that is always alight there points to God's continued presence. Priests and licensed members of the community take this reserved sacrament to those at home and in hospital who are too frail to come to the cathedral. Love bids us all welcome after all.

Our cathedral is a place to pray, a place to know God's forgiveness, a place to be fed with the body and blood of Christ.

> Love bade me welcome: yet my soul drew back,
> Guilty of dust and sin.
> But quick-eyed Love, observing me grow slack
> From my first entrance in,
> Drew nearer to me, sweetly questioning
> If I lacked anything.
>
> "A guest," I answered, "worthy to be here":
> Love said, "You shall be he."

CHAPTER 26

The spirituality of a cathedral—the flags

The cathedral bells rang a half-muffled quarter peal to help us remember those who died in the attack at a mosque in Christchurch just a few weeks ago. A solitary bell rang the "nine tailors", three times three rings together with rings for the number of the age of the one who died, 99 rings in all, to honour Bishop Bruce Rosier at his funeral on Ash Wednesday. The bells ring before each Sunday morning Choral Eucharist and after many weddings. The bells tell the city of Adelaide that something has happened, something is happening, something worthy of their attention, inviting the people of the city to worship, to mourn, to celebrate, to enter our cathedral doors. As the spires, reaching to the sky, point not only to God who we know in Christ and worship here in word and sacrament, music and in the company of strangers and friends, the spires remind the city that this cathedral is here, inviting them in. This cathedral, known across the cricket-loving world, by the "Cathedral end" of the Adelaide Oval, belongs not just to the beloved in the faith, but to the city, to the world.

This evening, in the final of our sermon series exploring the spirituality of St Peter's Cathedral in its 150th year, we symbolize our connection with the world by pondering the place of the flags. On 10 September 2011, the Governor-General, as Commander-in-Chief, presented the Queen's and Regimental Colours to 7th Battalion, the Royal Australian Regiment (7RAR) at the Torrens Parade Ground, Adelaide. Within days of this event, our cathedral was filled with soldiers, members of the 7RAR, who had come to lay up their old colours. Their old flag was to find its resting place in this cathedral under a window which portrays Christ on his cross. Bill Goodes, whose Spirituality Tour of the cathedral has so guided me in the writing of this series, deserves to be quoted in full about this window: "This is variously known as the 'Pope window' after its gifting by William Pope, a foundation Cathedral Warden, in honour of the three bishops with whom he worked, the 'Crucifixion window', or even the 'Love of God window'. The figure of the suffering Christ is at the centre of the window as it is at the centre of so much of Christianity—and this centrality is pictured in the figures by which the crucifix is surrounded. At the feet of Jesus is the scroll stating 'God so loved the world', while alongside him are the figures of the Old Testament prophets whose writings foreshadowed the cross." It is worth mentioning at this point that William Pope is just one of the many, many benefactors without whom this cathedral would not be standing, let alone adorned with so much beauty, beauty pointing in so many ways to the story of God who we know in Christ.

A cathedral is a place for military services and also for services for the state. State funerals take place here, organized with the detail and precision that only the military could surpass. Funerals are held for friends and strangers. Those close to our community will often have their ashes interred in the beautiful memorial garden planted lovingly in the shadow of the cross mirroring the Cross of Sacrifice across King William Road. Memorial services take place here, too. Late in 2013, we organized a powerful memorial service for Nelson Mandela who died on 5 December of that year. We gathered in leaders from not only different denominations from the Christian Church but also leaders from other world faiths, all working together to honour the man whose words "As I walked out the door toward the gate that would lead to my freedom I knew if I didn't leave my bitterness and hatred behind, I'd still be in prison" inspire many as they reflect on the struggle that is forgiveness.

A couple of years ago on United Nations Peace Day, we gathered leaders of many world faiths who prayed together on our nave platform at a service when our city's Independent Theatre Company inspired us with readings about war and peace. Our cathedral hosts many art forms—drama, the fine arts and, of course, music. In this way, we welcome in many who may not be of our faith but who find their lives nurtured and inspired by drama, art and music. Many in our city who may not necessarily assent to the Christian faith, experience Good Friday as a day on which they feel called to spend time in reflection. We honour this truth, on Good Friday at 3 o'clock in the afternoon each year, when the cathedral musicians put on a concert of music for reflection, in which Allegri's *Miserere* is often sung.

Funerals are held here for those we know well and for strangers. A baby who I will call Amelia, though that is not her name, and her twin sister were born prematurely at 26 weeks. After 18 months' struggle for life in the Women's and Children's Hospital, Amelia died. Her parents rang our office for help with her funeral. We had not known the family at all. We know them now. Amelia's funeral took place in this cathedral, and we attended her burial at a cemetery close to the family's home. Each year on the anniversary of her death, the family come to pray, to talk, to remember, to grieve a little more, to hold on to faith. Funerals for friends and strangers take place here.

So do weddings. When one of the cathedral clergy meets with a couple to discuss their wedding, we gently inquire what brought them here, often to a place they have not yet entered. "I've driven past this building so often and, since I was a little girl, I wanted to be married here," I have heard a bride say on more than one occasion. We do need one member of the couple to be baptized for an Anglican wedding to take place, but often their connection with our faith is just a whisper. The building has called them and only God will know how they will be nurtured in that faith by their conversations with cathedral clergy and staff and the sharing of their wedding ceremony with us. On occasion, couples return with their children, asking us to welcome them in baptism.

Near the flags is a place for the lighting of candles, one of two places permanently set up for this in the cathedral. Another is near the Lady Chapel beneath an icon of St Nicholas. A kneeler is placed there for private prayers for those close to the heart of the one who prays, often for those who are suffering or dying.

What are we doing when we light candles and pray for those we love dearly or those who have been injured far away? Michael Mayne, former Dean of Westminster Abbey, wrote in *Pray, Love, Remember*, the book from which the idea for this sermon series came:

> None of us is immune to pain. We get sick; we die. We lose those who mean the most to us in the world. There is no such thing as divine protection. Jesus died an agonizing death. So what did he prove? He died to prove the seemingly foolish claim that the

> self-giving love that shaped his own life is what lies at the heart of the universe; and that if you would name the unimaginable presence that informs it and holds it in being, then you must use the name "Abba", the intimate name a child gives its father. And that life is learning to trust that these things are so; and learning to grow in that self-giving love.[1]

When we light candles we place into this love the people, the situations, the struggles for which we pray.

Each week at Choral Evensong on a Wednesday, we light candles for peace whilst the anthem is being sung by the choir. Not long ago a man walked into a Manchester concert venue and, blowing himself up, killed scores of innocent human beings and injured many more. A man walked into our cathedral during that candle lighting service the following Wednesday. The service was well under way and the man joined us. When the service ended and the organ was being played, the man who had walked into our cathedral came forward and lit a candle, and placed his candle in the bowl with the many other lighted candles, and he took a photo of the bowl and the prayer for the Manchester victims we placed by the candles. He came over to me at the side door of our cathedral, and he shook my hand and he said this. "I am the director of the cathedral in Manchester. I will send this photo to my Dean. Please tell your Dean. Thank you for doing this."

In so many ways this place welcomes in the world.

What are we doing here in St Peter's Cathedral? This place where love bids us welcome? Michael Mayne asks this question of his abbey:

> What is this space for? It is where human beings, in all our marvellous diversity, may sometimes engage with the transcendent; for the space we have inherited is not just any old space, but a holy space, the place where past generations have met in search of that encounter between the seen and the unseen.[2]

---

1 Michael Mayne, *Pray, Love, Remember* (London: Darton, Longman & Todd, 1999), p. 12.

2 Mayne, *Pray, Love, Remember*, p. 107.

Our witness here in this cathedral, is that this "unseen" is God. God who shines forth in Jesus Christ, God whose story is told here in word and sacrament, music, drama and art, wood and glass and stone, God who we know in the presence of the body of Christ gathered here, God who through this cathedral makes us welcome:

Love bade me welcome: yet my soul drew back,
    Guilty of dust and sin.
But quick-eyed Love, observing me grow slack
    From my first entrance in,
Drew nearer to me, sweetly questioning
    If I lacked anything.

"A guest," I answered, "worthy to be here":
    Love said, "You shall be he."
"I, the unkind, ungrateful? Ah, my dear,
    I cannot look on thee."
Love took my hand, and smiling did reply,
    "Who made the eyes but I?"

"Truth, Lord; but I have marred them; let my shame
    Go where it doth deserve."
"And know you not," says Love, "who bore the blame?"
    "My dear, then I will serve."
"You must sit down," says Love, "and taste my meat."
    So I did sit and eat.

PART 6

Jesus—Windows on his story

CHAPTER 27

Held in the story of God

What have we come to see? What have we come to hear?

We have entered the cathedral this Christmas Day, expectant. We may come here often; we may come only once a year; it doesn't matter. We have come.

What have we brought with us? The smell of smoke from the bushfires that are raging across our country, the images of fires burning out of control, the knowledge that many, many of our fellow South Australians, fellow Australians are now without their homes and a few . . . including two firefighters, fathers of little children . . . have lost their lives. Did we see the photo of those firefighters' helmets on the plaque surrounded with flowers? Those brave young men who will not see Christmas Day? Did we see the images of firefighters lying exhausted on the ground, knowing that they would still be needed to fight fires for the days, weeks, months ahead?

Have we brought worry with us? Worry about our planet and the warming that now seems impossible to deny. Worry about the plastics that clog our seas, plastics that we struggle so greatly to break away from using. Worry about our family, perhaps, or a dear friend, facing illness or frailty, or grief. Have we lost someone we love dearly this last year? Have we brought grief with us?

Or have we brought joy? Was a child born in our family; was some study done well; have we treasured family and friends so deeply this year we have come thinking in joy and gratitude about the blessing of their presence in our lives? Have we found our vocation, the work or the way of living that brings us to life, is that what we've brought this Christmas morning?

For we bring our life story here. As we walk through the doors, we bring our life story here. And what do we encounter? What have we come to see? What have we come to hear? Something of God's story, I think.

Just as we have, the shepherds came all those years ago.

The shepherds are living in the fields, keeping watch over their flock by night, so the story goes. An angel from God comes, with the glory of God shining about them, and the shepherds are terrified. People are usually terrified when they sense God's presence in an unexpected way, when an angel comes. The word for angel in the language of the Gospel stories means "messenger". God is telling us something when an angel comes, and we are always shaken by that. Be careful, angels don't always have golden wings. They might not have wings at all, but we'll sense God's presence. We'll sense love addressing us, grace enfolding us. The angel says to the shepherds, "Do not be afraid." It is the first thing angels always say. Then they tell their news and they guide us as to what we are to do, what God would have us do. "I am bringing you good news of great joy for all the people: to you is born this day in the city of David a Saviour, who is the Messiah, the Lord. This will be a sign for you: you will find a child wrapped in bands of cloth and lying in a manger." The angels sing to the shepherds about the glory of God and about peace coming, peace coming to the whole earth. Once the angels have left, the shepherds go, go quickly, and find things just as the angels have said. There in the stable are Mary and Joseph, and the baby lying in the manger.

Just as we have come into the cathedral this Christmas morning, the shepherds come.

And what they see is that *God has come*. God has come to live among us. God has come to see *us*, to hear *us*, to dwell among *us*. God has come as a baby to show us that where we are little and vulnerable and new, God is there too. God has come through the courage and faith of Mary and Joseph to show us that when we struggle to find courage and to have faith, God is with us. God has come in the most unlikely place, a stable in a village in a faraway country amidst poor and unimportant people to show us that wherever we are and whoever we are, God arrives amongst us.

We might worry, though, that after we've journeyed to see this holy thing, we will find the manger empty, just a trough where the oxen and the sheep feed. Imagine that as we approach from a distance the stable looks empty. When the bushfires are raging out of control, when illness strikes one we love, when we wonder how to hope, the stable looks empty. Imagine the loneliness of it, the hopelessness of it. Then, imagine coming closer, and seeing the baby there. Imagine the shock, the questions in our minds. Imagine the wonder, the hope. Imagine the possibility that God has come. That God sees and God loves. That God is living with us, standing by us, guiding us on. God is there in times of bushfire, in the struggle to care for our planet, in times of illness, in vales of grief, in times of joy. Might we look into the manger, and see the baby, and wonder.

Could it be? Could it be that God inhabited this earth for a time, lived and died and rose again in Jesus, the one whose name means saviour, so that we know that God inhabits this earth now, is with us now?

What has God come to see, to hear? God has come for us, for all of us, and the dear earth that God created for us to call our home.

We heard of shepherds travelling to visit a stable. What did they find there, those shepherds? As they gazed at that baby lying in a manger all that time ago? What do we find? That stable scene in Bethlehem is as earthly and broken as any place on our planet at any time in its history. It is as earthly and broken as our time and our place. It is woven with images of God. Angels and stars and wise men on camels bearing gifts that point to the divinity and humanity of that baby. God came down from heaven that night, the Word was made flesh and dwelt among us there in that stable, Emmanuel, God with us, embraced a human life that we humans might know that God holds each and every one of our lives, and the life of this beloved planet, in his embrace. We come to this story struggling as Mary and Joseph and every other member of its cast did with the extraordinary call and action of God. That God brings hope into this broken world. That God is deeply in love with this utterly earthly place.

What have we come to see? What have we come to hear?

Our story held. The story of our own life, the life of our loved ones, our community and our world, held. Held in the story of God. God who loves, God who walks with us, God who brings healing and peace. Yes. God is deeply in love with this utterly earthly place. God is born in this utterly earthly place.

CHAPTER 28

Simeon's song

As we gather for Choral Evensong this evening, rejoicing in the presence of the choir, how wonderful it is to begin the service with the introit by Johannes Eccard, "When to the temple Mary went". How wonderful to hear again the psalm chanted and the canticles sung. It is fitting that this evening is the feast at which we remember the story of one of those canticles, the Feast of the Presentation of Christ in the Temple. In this scene, from Luke 2, the scene remembered in our introit, we hear the story of when, not long after Jesus is born, the time comes for the family's purification according to the law of Moses, and Mary and Joseph bring Jesus up to Jerusalem to present him to God, offering as a sacrifice a pair of turtle-doves or two young pigeons. It is a story of people of devout faith, living out the sacraments of that faith in their time and place.

Following the circumcision of Jesus, the story of which is told in the previous verses of Luke's Gospel, two further religious acts are required of Joseph and Mary—the redemption of the first-born son and his mother's purification. Steeped in the stories of their faith, the Jewish first-born children were consecrated to the Lord as a reminder of the story of the Exodus, when all the first-born children and animals were killed except the Israelite children who were "passed over" by the Lord. They were reminded of their salvation story.

Joseph and Mary, though, find greater blessing in their visit to the temple for these sacred rites, than those they expected. They find encounters with two people of profound faith, two people who, nurtured by their faith in God, keep watch for signs of God's action in history:

> Now there is a man in Jerusalem whose name is Simeon; this man is righteous and devout, looking forward to the consolation of

> Israel, and the Holy Spirit rests on him. It has been revealed to him by the Holy Spirit that he will not see death before he had seen the Lord's Messiah. Guided by the Spirit, Simeon comes into the temple; and when the parents bring in the child Jesus, to do for him what is customary under the law, Simeon takes him in his arms. (Luke 2:25–8)

The Spirit is ever present in these few verses. The Holy Spirit rests on Simeon. The Holy Spirit reveals to him that he will see the Messiah before he dies, and this day, the Spirit guides him into the temple. There is no doubt that this encounter is God's doing. A blessing for Simeon and then, how much more so a blessing for Mary and Joseph and all who hear his words. All, including us, years later, who hear his words. Hear his words sung.

For Simeon, through the Holy Spirit, then guides that child's parents. Simeon takes Jesus in his arms and praises God, saying,

> Master, now you are dismissing your servant in peace,
>   according to your word;
> for my eyes have seen your salvation,
>   which you have prepared in the presence of all peoples,
> a light for revelation to the Gentiles
>   and for glory to your people Israel. (Luke 2:29–32)

Simeon's words do not end there. He also blesses Mary and Joseph and then he turns to Mary and speaks to her, speaks to her of Jesus' vocation and her own. "This child is destined for the falling and rising of many in Israel," he says. Some will fall, some will rise in response to Jesus. "And the inner thoughts of many will be revealed." Jesus' presence will expose who we are, and Mary is told of the pain of it for her, "a sword will pierce your own soul too" (Luke 2:34–5). These are more words for her to ponder in her heart, to put with the angel Gabriel's words to her and the shepherds' words to her.

Then there is Anna. The prophet who is also a person of devout faith, worshipping in the temple night and day who, when Mary and Joseph and Jesus come, praises God and speaks about the child to all who are looking for the redemption of Jerusalem.

Yes, the Nunc Dimittis is a blessing for Mary and Joseph and all who hear Simeon's words sung. A result of reflection on this story by scholars and musicians and ordinary people of faith, this story of people of devout faith, living out the sacraments of that faith in their time and place.

During this time of pandemic, which for many has meant coming to church, cathedral or indeed temple has not been possible, many churches and cathedrals have nurtured their own people of devout faith with services and music and talks online. I found myself watching one of the canons of Canterbury Cathedral, Emma Pennington, this week, speaking in a series entitled "Pathways into Prayer". Her talk was about *lectio divina*, holy reading, a way of spending time with a scripture passage that helps us listen to God, spend time with God, who would speak to us, reach out to us in scripture. Canon Emma used a word that I had not thought of before in the context of this way with scripture, a beautiful word that, for me, gave insight into what might happen when we allow scripture to reach us.

Lectio divina can be thought of as having four stages: *lectio*—reading, *meditatio*—meditating, *oratio*—prayer and *contemplation*—contemplate. It was about the second stage, *meditatio*, that our Canterbury Cathedral Canon said the following: She encouraged us to:

> Lightly hold the text in our mind and allow the Holy Spirit to guide us to what jumps out or, how I like to imagine it, shimmers in the text for us. This may be a word or a sentence but once it comes into the forefront of your mind thinking it, holding it there, and allowing it to unfold itself as you ponder or meditate upon it.[1]

Lightly hold the text in our mind and allow the Holy Spirit to guide us to what jumps out or, how I like to imagine it, shimmers in the text for us.

---

1 Canterbury Cathedral, "Pathways into Prayer" Lectio Divina with Canon Emma Pennington on YouTube.

I thought the word "shimmer" was very beautiful. What is the word or sentence in a small passage of scripture on which we are reflecting that shimmers for us?

Lectio divina is about keeping watch, listening for God, about noting what, through the Holy Spirit, shimmers for us. In a way, this is just what each one of the characters in the story of the Presentation in the Temple have spent their lives doing . . . keeping watch, listening for God, noticing what shimmers. Simeon, whose song is the Nunc Dimittis, guided by the Holy Spirit, watches not only scripture but life, events, the happenings of each day as those days pass him by.

Simeon is ready to notice a baby. This baby shimmered for Simeon. Jesus shimmered for Simeon. Guided by the Spirit, Simeon, who was accustomed to keeping watch for the sign of God's salvation, noticed when that salvation came into the temple in his mother's arms. Then he spoke.

What shimmers for us in this story? As we gather in the presence of music and liturgy and one another's presence, conscious of the extraordinary blessing that we can do so. What shimmers for us? As schools return and ordinary life resumes and we know that in many places in the world, for so many, this is not so. What shimmers for us? As we remember the devotion of the firefighters who saved so many homes just days ago in our own Adelaide Hills and we think of the grief of the two families whose homes did not survive. What shimmers for us?

In a story of devotion and keeping watch and then speaking out when the one who has kept watch for so long knows that God is at work. In a way that is what our life of faith is all about. Giving God time, be it reflecting on scripture using *lectio divina* or some other way of holy reading, be it allowing the beautiful music of our cathedral choir and our cathedral organ to waft over us, be it walking in the bush. Giving God time, that guided by the Holy Spirit as Simeon and Anna were, we might find that something shimmers and we, too, will know ourselves truly blessed.

CHAPTER 29

Layers removed

Rowan Williams, in the book that is guiding our cathedral community through Lent, writes this of Lent:

> Layers removed: it's another image for what Lent and Passiontide are all about. We try to let some kind of sharp, cleansing wind blow through the fog of idleness and selfishness, so that the landscape of our spirits stands more clearly. Not that it's always a pretty sight . . . but it's only when the vague drifting muddle of the way we usually think about ourselves is blown away by the Spirit that we see the underlying contours—the deep needs, the ingrained resistances, the aching hopes and loves.[1]

Layers removed.

I guess this is what Jesus experienced at his baptism and then in his time in the wilderness. We are in Mark's Gospel, and we know the accounts will be brief. No detail of the three temptations with which Satan challenges Jesus as in Matthew and Luke's Gospel. Just two sentences on which to ponder Jesus' 40 days of that cleansing wind of which Rowan Williams writes:

> The Spirit immediately drives him out into the wilderness. He is in the wilderness for forty days, tempted by Satan; and he is with the wild beasts; and the angels wait on him. (Mark 1:12–13)

1 Rowan Williams, *Candles in the Dark: Faith, Hope and Love in a Time of Pandemic* (London: SPCK, 2020), p. 5.

The writers of the lectionary which guides our readings each Sunday clearly think that two sentences is not enough for a Gospel reading and so we have the story of Jesus' baptism and the story of Jesus' proclamation of the coming of the kingdom as well.

Layers removed.

These words might well describe what Jesus experienced at his baptism too. We don't know how clearly he saw his identity. We know from Luke's Gospel that at the age of 12 he knew himself deeply at home in his Father's house learning from the rabbis. Then there is a great gap in the story. Until now.

> Just as Jesus comes up out of the water, he sees the heavens torn apart and the Spirit descending like a dove on him. And a voice comes from heaven, "You are my Son, the Beloved; with you I am well pleased". (Mark 1:10–11)

Through what one writer described as a "gracious gash in the universe",[2] the spirit descends on Jesus, into Jesus, and he knows who he is. God's Beloved Son. The one with whom God is well pleased.

Knowing this is not enough. Jesus is a human being who must walk the earth in full knowledge of human frailty. There is no time to bask in the joy of God's words to him, in the Spirit's blessing. Immediately (it is always immediately in Mark's Gospel, remember) the Spirit drives him into the wilderness. Immediately the truth of being fully human is inflicted on him and he is tempted by Satan. The wild beasts come and yet there is also the presence of the angels. Jesus is not alone here, and neither, when we ponder our Lent, are we.

Did Jesus also find himself exposed to the sharp, cleansing wind of which Rowan Williams writes? Did he know the vague drifting muddle of the way we usually think about ourselves being blown away by the Spirit? Did he find himself exposed by his deep needs, his ingrained resistances, his aching hopes and loves? Then, as the angels waited on him, did he, in a way that none of us could manage, breathe deeply,

---

2 J. Marcus, quoted in John Shea, *Eating with the Bridegroom* (Collegeville, MN: Liturgical Press, 2005), p. 79.

and turning towards God, stay utterly true to his vocation? He had to experience this wilderness though. He had to know what we know. How could he accompany us in our Lent otherwise?

What of us, then? How might we allow the sharp cleansing wind to blow through our fogs of idleness and selfishness? Harsh words, really, but we would expect no less than the truth from Rowan Williams.

We are encouraged in Lent to give up things and take other things on. So, let's wonder about that. What is it that gets in the way of God? What do we think makes us worthwhile, makes us beloved, that is not of God? It's probably not chocolate, nor even a good red wine. Though there's nothing wrong with giving those up if this helps us to reflect. We are encouraged to ponder prayer and fasting and almsgiving as our Lenten practice, after all. What do we love that is not God, or given us by God to love? What are our golden calves, the things we worship that are not God? Might we notice and put them to one side for this Lenten time, our 40 days?

And what might we take up? How might we allow the sharp, cleansing wind to blow through the fog of idleness and selfishness, so that the landscape of our spirits stands more clearly? It sounds painful, sounds like the wild beasts, but the angels are with us too. The spirit will not put us through what we cannot bear. And mightn't it be a relief? To look with God at this vague drifting muddle of the way we usually think about ourselves? Because we surely know, if we're honest, don't we? We surely know about the muddle and about the sins. We know about the ways of being that we just would love to break and yet never quite manage to grow out of. We surely know. Mightn't the cleansing wind, the spirit that descends on us through the gracious gash in the universe, be a relief? Do you mean you know, God, what I'm really like and you're still here longing to keep company with my deep needs, my ingrained resistances, my aching hopes and loves? Longing to forgive me and set me free?

Our psalm encourages us to ponder in God's company:

> Make me to know your ways, O Lord;
>   teach me your paths.
> Lead me in your truth, and teach me,
>   for you are the God of my salvation;

for you I wait all day long.
Be mindful of your mercy, O Lord, and of your steadfast love,
    for they have been from of old.
Do not remember the sins of my youth or my transgressions;
    according to your steadfast love remember me,
for your goodness' sake, O Lord! (Psalm 25:4–7)

Does our psalm guide us in our calling this Lent? Are we to spend time pondering in God's company? Remembering our sins and then hearing God's forgiveness, being mindful of God's mercy and steadfast love, as the psalm puts it. Asking God to teach us God's paths and to lead us in God's truth.

I guess, in the end, what God longs for is a little time, a little of our time. Each day in Lent, if we can manage it. Can we give ten minutes, perhaps, or more, each Lenten day? Could we sit in our favourite place, with our favourite words of scripture or poetry, or silently gazing at a tree, or an icon, or the waves of the sea? Sitting or walking, it doesn't matter. I think what God longs for is a little of our time. We will find ourselves changed by that. Prayer, I sometimes think, is like waves on a rock. Only after days and weeks and years of the waves rolling in over a rock will the rock be changed, its contours shaped by the movement of the sea. Prayer is like that, I think. So, what God longs for is a little of our time.

We'll find we sense the company of one who looks kindly upon us. The one who promised a rainbow in the sky and never to give up on us again. The presence of the one who sees all our sins, yes, and all our struggles and all our hopes and all the ways in which we bless one another. Yes, we'll find ourselves in the presence of one who looks kindly upon us.

So, we will finish our thoughts this First Sunday in Lent, with some gentler words, I think. Michael Mayne, the former Dean of Westminster Abbey, spoke of Lent in this way:

> On Ash Wednesday some of us have ash placed on our foreheads with the words: "Remember you are dust and to dust you shall return" . . . Yet Lent is not a bleak, forbidding time, but a very positive and optimistic remembering of who and what we truly are. "Dust", yes, but dust that dreams of glory. Dust that has

been claimed by God. Dust that has a deep aching sense both of its mortality and of its reaching after the God glimpsed in Jesus whom one day we shall see face to face. Lent is a time for remembering where our true home lies, and for setting our face once again in that direction.[3]

3 Michael Mayne, *Dust that Dreams of Glory* (Norwich: Canterbury Press, 2017), p. 7.

CHAPTER 30

We wish to see Jesus

In the twelfth chapter of John's Gospel, from which our passion reading is taken, after Jesus has entered Jerusalem on a donkey to the cries of Hosannas from the crowd, some Greeks come to Jesus' disciple Philip and say, "Sir, we wish to see Jesus." Jesus says in response, "The hour has come . . . " (John 12:21,23)

It is on this day, Good Friday, that the hour has come, that we see who Jesus is. On Good Friday, in our cathedral, we sit at the foot of Jesus' cross. Accompanying one another as we keep watch in his dying, surrounded by the singing of the choir from the gallery, listening to words of the passion, gazing at the wood of this cross towering over us draped in red silk, his life poured out for us.

As we sit at the foot of Jesus' cross, the stories of suffering in our world echo in our minds. The stories of pandemic, of a planet groaning in pain, the horrifying stories of Ukraine.

The pandemic wrought by Coronavirus ID number 19 has plagued our world for over two years now. We hear that some children struggle to recognize facial expressions because so much of their formative years have been spent with people in masks. We know that thanks to the fierce skill and determination of scientists, vaccines have been developed so that many more won't die when the virus strikes, but those vaccines have not been shared equally across the world. The damage wrought by the virus in those parts of the world is still dire. We know that across the world, many of the elderly in nursing homes have had their dementia accelerated and their mobility stifled as they are confined to their rooms, sheltering from the spread of the virus but unable to see those who love them and remind them who they are.

The signs of our planet's climate change are more and more evident on our own shores, but did we hear Simon Kofe, the foreign minister of Tuvalu, speak at the time of the COP26 summit, a summit committed to working to stem the fierce tide of climate change? He was standing in the sea. The shore of his island behind him. His lectern—the lectern on which sat the words of his speech to those gathered in Glasgow at the COP26 summit—also stood in the sea. His nation's flag was fluttering in the breeze. "Climate change and sea level rise are deadly existential threats to Tuvalu and low-lying Atol countries," Simon Kofe said. "We are sinking, but so is everyone else. In Tuvalu we are living the realities of climate change and sea level rise."[1] In a radio interview on our own Radio National Breakfast programme, though, Simon Kofe posed a question for experts in international law: "If a country is submerged, does it still have nation status?"[2] Do we still exist in the eyes of international law, he was asking. Do we still exist in God's eyes, are we still seen, he might ask the dying Jesus.

And then there is Ukraine. It might seem difficult to believe that in a world created by one who loves us this much, we need to have international laws to govern human behaviour at time of war. Laws that have been brutally violated in Ukraine.

The world saw the atrocities in Larysa Savenko's suburban Ukrainian neighbourhood days before she did.

The 72-year-old was still hiding in her house in the town of Bucha, near the capital Kyiv, just days ago when apocalyptic scenes of burnt-out military vehicles, ruined homes and muddy chaos on Vokzal'na Street became the latest defining images of the war.

Ms Savenko was holed up in her shed for five weeks in the freezing cold, with her son and a homeless lodger, as Russian forces occupied the street on the road to Kyiv.

"We couldn't go out, everything around was on fire," Ms Savenko said.

1 <https://opecfund.org/news/small-island-developing-states-when-everything-is-at-stake>, accessed 21 May 2024.

2 <https://www.abc.net.au/radionational/programs/breakfast/tuvalu-could-be-uninhabitable-in-50-years-due-to-climate-change/13626284>, accessed 28 February 2024.

"There was shooting everywhere, so we got out through the kitchen window and hid in a cellar." Many residents were trapped without access to power, water or food. Every few days, Ms Savenko scurried through her yard to the house next door to feed her neighbour, who was unable to walk.

Retreating Russian soldiers had left the corpses of civilians strewn across the streets near Ms Savenko's home.

These are the stories of the suffering of our world that we place at the foot of Jesus' cross. He hears, he sees and as he dies, he speaks. Seven Last Words we find in the Gospel accounts, words that he speaks to those before him. In his words, we find the love of God addressing suffering humanity in all its times and all its places.

"Father, forgive them; for they do not know what they are doing," Jesus says to the soldiers who stand before him, the ones who have robbed him of his life (Luke 23:24). Jesus looks at the ones who nailed him to his cross and, in all the physical and spiritual pain that surrounds him, he utters these words of forgiveness.

There is a story sometimes told about God's forgiveness, about God needing a sacrifice. I do not believe that Jesus is placating an angry Father God who needs a death to take away the world's sin. This is not what is meant when we say Jesus died to take away the sins of the world. Jesus died forgiving. This was, of course, an event in time and space. A dying man speaking words at a particular time, in a particular place, forgiving particular people. But it was more than that. As the veil of the temple is torn in two at the death of Jesus, his words send shock waves through all creation, waves of forgiveness for all time and in every place. Can we imagine this? Forgiveness for all the sins of our world? The awful sins of our time and place. When we struggle to contemplate God's forgiveness of the soldiers of our time and place, we might wonder . . . can we imagine God's forgiveness of our own sin?

Jesus speaks to his mother, a mother who is to lose her son and so her home. "Woman, here is your son," he says as she stands with the disciple he loves, "here is your mother" (John 19:26–7). As we contemplate the people of Ukraine and so many others made homeless through war and suffering, we hear Jesus making a home for his mother. Homes are made in the most difficult of circumstances, made in Jesus' spirit poured out on the cross, like Larysa Savenko's home for five weeks in the freezing cold in a shed, with her son and a homeless lodger, as Russian forces occupied the street on the road to Kyiv. A home that extended to her neighbour, unable to walk, whom to feed Larysa risked her life. Homes made for the millions who have fled Ukraine, Syria, Afghanistan, victims of human violence as Jesus' mother was, a victim of the violence meted out on her son.

Then there are the stories of our beloved ones, the beloved of our community who have died . . . not from the virus that plagues us, not from fire or flood, not from the violence of war, but from the illnesses that strike us and the frailty of age. The stories of our beloved ones and our struggle to learn to live without their nearness, without their voices speaking with us, with memory and the fierceness of our love for them leading us on. He sees us ache in it.

Jesus sees and he speaks. "I thirst," Jesus says (John 19:28). The Word made flesh, Jesus incarnate, knows the struggle of humanity, knows hunger and thirst, knows the suffering our physical need brings. He knows our longing for meaning in it. Jesus speaks the truth of it, inhabits the reality of it. He knows death in it and knows that sometimes there is despair.

Dying on his cross, he sees and he speaks:

> My God, my God, why have you forsaken me? (Mark 15:34)

He was so close to his Father, the one he called Abba. All his love and healing, all his teaching and delighting in the company of sinners, all of it flowed from his closeness to God. In his dying, that closeness was gone, and we can only wonder at the terror of it, that at the very moment he needed his Father's closeness most, he felt abandoned. There was only suffering in the Father. The theologian Jürgen Moltmann wrote the most helpful words I have read on this:

> The Father delivers up his Son on the cross in order to be the Father of those who are delivered up. In the forsakenness of the Son the Father also forsakes himself. In the surrender of the Son the Father also surrenders himself . . . The Father who abandons

> him and delivers him up suffers the death of the Son in the infinite grief of love. . . . The Son suffers dying, the Father suffers the death of the Son.[3]
>
> The deep community of will between Jesus and his God and Father is now expressed precisely at the point of their deepest separation in the godforsaken and accursed death of Jesus on the cross.[4]

In his dying, Jesus prays. Prays the words he had prayed throughout his life, the words of his faith, the psalms. Prays his despair in Psalm 22 and prays the night prayer, Psalm 31, with his last breath. Helping us know that in our suffering and in our hour, our hour of death, that praying never ceases. That the dying Jesus is there praying with us. "Father, into thy hands I commend my spirit." He prays.

We come looking for Jesus, this Good Friday. Tentatively, almost in fear we come. Somehow, though, it seems that in him, as we gaze at the cross, we are found. It is he who finds us. In all the echoes of the stories of suffering in our world, Jesus sees us, hears us, addresses us, names us. It is us and all God's beloved creation who are found, who are seen.

The hour has come.

Behold Jesus dying on the cross. Behold love dying on the cross, behold God.

---

3 Jürgen Moltmann, *The Crucified God* (London: SCM Press, 1974), p. 251.

4 Moltmann, *The Crucified God*, p. 252.

CHAPTER 31

Startled by Jesus

During Lent, our cathedral community has reflected on Rowan Williams' book *Candles in the Dark*. Rowan Williams wrote the following about Easter:

> One of the things that Easter declares is that our world of time and change has been transformed by the event of Jesus's resurrection. When we say that Jesus is risen, we mean that there is no sense in which he belongs to the past; his life is never over. When we celebrate the Eucharist, we don't put flowers on a memorial slab; we meet a living and active presence. And if his life is not over in time, neither is it confined in space. The Easter stories in the New Testament suggest that, again and again, the disciples are startled to meet Jesus, he turns up in unexpected places.[1]

... again and again, the disciples are startled to meet Jesus, he turns up in unexpected places.

So, this evening, on the Second Sunday of Easter, I thought we would wonder a little about the startled-ness of those disciples . . . and whether there are times when we might be startled, startled by Jesus' presence, God's presence too.

Our New Testament reading is from the first verses of Luke 24. This passage is Luke's version of the story of the empty tomb. Knowing how the story goes, it is difficult for us to put ourselves in the places of the women coming to the tomb to anoint Jesus' body with spices and ointments. They

---

1 Rowan Williams, *Candles in the Dark: Faith, Hope and Love in a Time of Pandemic* (London: SPCK, 2020), pp. 10–11.

were expecting a closed tomb, they were expecting a body laid there. They were expecting tears and a final farewell to this one who had given life to them, hope to them. They were expecting death.

> They find the stone rolled away from the tomb, and when they go in, they do not find the body. While they are perplexed about this, suddenly two men in dazzling clothes stand beside them. The women are terrified and bowed their faces to the ground, but the men said to them, "Why do you look for the living among the dead? He is not here, but has risen." (Luke 24:2–5)

They are startled. It is not that they understand, do you see, this is not about understanding. It is about new sight. It is about not seeing what they were certain they would see. A body, a death. And seeing, hearing, about life. The women go and tell the eleven apostles. Only Peter responds to the women. In Luke's version of the story, Peter gets up and runs to the tomb; stooping and looking in, he sees the linen cloths by themselves; then he goes home, amazed at what had happened. Startled too. Peter too does not understand anything. The world is changed.

Rowan Williams says that "our world of time and change has been transformed by the event of Jesus's resurrection". The women, Peter, the disciples, could not have articulated that, certainly not that day, perhaps never. They were transformed. They were startled. In the snippets of stories that we read in the four Gospel accounts we see Jesus meeting the disciples in different places, meeting their different needs—fear, doubt, guilt—every time transforming them.

The Old Testament has its startling stories too. This evening's Old Testament reading from the book of the prophet Ezekiel tells the story of the dry bones. Ezekiel tells the story:

> The hand of the LORD came upon me, and he brought me out by the spirit of the LORD and set me down in the middle of a valley; it was full of bones. He led me all round them; there were very many lying in the valley, and they were very dry. He said to me, "Mortal, can these bones live?" I answered, "O LORD God, you know." Then he said to me, "Prophesy to these bones, and say to

> them: O dry bones, hear the word of the Lord. Thus says the Lord God to these bones: I will cause breath to enter you, and you shall live. I will lay sinews on you, and will cause flesh to come upon you, and cover you with skin, and put breath in you, and you shall live; and you shall know that I am the Lord." (Ezekiel 37:1–6)

As the prophecy was told the bones came together, and then the sinews and then the flesh. There was no breath until the prophet prophesied again and then the breath came and the bones lived. The dry dead bones came to life. The point of it, as it related to the life of the people Israel, the point of it was that they came back to life. What they knew was that the Lord, the presence of the Lord, is in this giving of breath, this bringing to life. Where breath is given, where life is restored, it is the work of the Lord.

When we look on startled, when we listen, wondering almost in disbelief at such a prophecy, we might allow ourselves to wonder, to be startled, to know the presence of the Lord. As the women did, as Peter did. Not trying to understand. Just knowing that they were in the presence of the Lord, that only God, the one Jesus called Father, could have done this.

So, what of us? How might we be startled by the resurrection, this year, this Easter?

Our psalm, Psalm 115, helps us know what gets in the way, what gets in the way of being touched by the resurrection. The psalm speaks of idols, the idols of those who do not worship God. And it speaks with such insight:

> Wherefore shall the heathen say
> Where is now their God
> . . . Their idols are silver and gold
> even the work of men's hands.
> They have mouths, and speak not
> eyes have they, and see not.
> They have ears, and hear not
> noses have they, and smell not.
> They have hands, and handle not; feet have they, and walk not
> neither speak they through their throat.

> They that make them are like unto them
> and so are all such as put their trust in them. (Psalm 115:2,4–8)

It's not only the heathen who worship idols; we all do that at times. We all have things that we put in the place of God, when God gets too difficult, seems too far away. When we are baffled, puzzled, startled, lonely for God, perhaps.

Listen to what the psalm says of those who worship idols—the idols that have mouths that speak not, eyes that see not, ears that hear not . . . it says those who put their trust in idols are like those idols with mouths and eyes and ears that do not function, that neither speak, nor see, nor hear.

In the presence of resurrection truth, it is so easy to turn away. The psalm is hinting to us that we need to use all our senses, if you like. To see, to hear . . . to allow the resurrection stories to niggle away at us, to ponder them. For it may be that it is when we are walking on the beach that something of the stories will cause us to wonder. We may see them or hear them in a new light. It may be that when we are listening to the choir sing that the beauty of the music helps the newness of resurrection reach us. It may be that when we are struck by the kindness, an unexpected kindness, of another human being, that this kindness somehow has new life woven into it. Resurrection has many guises. The key is to allow it. The key is not to sit with our old idols, the things that seem easy to worship, with the unseeing eyes and the unhearing ears. The key is to allow the mystery of the resurrection stories to reach us; to allow a sense of the risen Jesus to encounter us; to find ourselves startled, as we meet Jesus turning up in unexpected places, as Rowan Williams said.

PART 7

Jesus—The stories he told

CHAPTER 32

Tears pouring down his cheeks

Praying for peace in the Middle East, the Archbishop of Canterbury stood outside Lambeth Palace in London, a Muslim community leader on one side and a Jewish community leader on the other side, speaking of peace, of the abhorrence of violence, in a bid to discourage "any form of hatred or violence" in the UK.

It was after this that the bombs fell on the Anglican hospital in Gaza killing hundreds of innocent men, women and children. Archbishop Welby wrote:

> I appeal again for hostages to be released and for civilians to be protected. I join the international call for all parties to grant immediate, safe humanitarian access into Gaza to prevent further loss of life. I pray again for the peace of Jerusalem, in solidarity with the Church in the Holy Land. I grieve with Israelis and Palestinians still mourning and in fear.
>
> In the name of Jesus Christ, I urge a different path—one that spares innocent lives and pursues justice, security and lasting peace for all.[1]

Religious leaders, any one of us, are not always so wise. Jesus found himself confronted by religious leaders who did not offer the same grief-stricken peaceful wisdom. As they do often in the Gospel stories, the leaders confronting Jesus in our reading this morning are trying to trap

---

1 <https://www.archbishopofcanterbury.org/news/news-and-statements/archbishop-canterbury-appeals-end-bloodshed-after-atrocious-attack-gaza>, accessed 1 March 2024.

him. They ask a simple question, really, a black-and-white, Yes-or-No, question:

> Is it lawful to pay taxes to the emperor, or not? (Matthew 22:17)

They call him Teacher and they sarcastically say that he is sincere and teaches the way of God in accordance with truth, and shows deference to no one, favouring no one. He points to the truth, all right, but not as they expect.

The trap set by these leaders is clever. If Jesus says "No", in speaking against the emperor, he will be speaking against Rome. The Herodians have been sent along to witness Jesus' answer. Herod is in power with the Romans' approval, so they will have grounds to charge him. If Jesus says "Yes", he will discredit himself as a prophet and those who follow him will fall away. Those who follow Jesus hate the Roman taxes—all creation belongs to God and the taxes were onerous; those who collected them took part in bribery and cheating. Such an answer would contradict much of his teaching.

He doesn't answer "Yes" or "No". In his reflection with those who try to trap him, we see the one who is from God reflect on questions that challenge. He looks into their hearts and names them as hypocrites and then he ponders the context. In this case, he asks for a Roman coin.

"Show me the coin used for the tax," he says. So, they bring him a denarius. He says to them, "Whose head is this, and whose title?" They answer, "The Emperor's." Then he says to them, "Give therefore to the Emperor the things that are the Emperor's, and to God the things that are God's."

He doesn't answer the question; he ponders hearts and context.

The same day some Sadducees come to question Jesus. They do not believe in the resurrection. They hope to gain his agreement by telling a story that would seek to use logic to trap him. If a woman marries seven brothers, one by one as each die, who will be her husband in the resurrection? The resurrection is not logical, they say!

Jesus again looks into their hearts.

"You are wrong," he says, "because you know neither the scriptures nor the power of God." He continues, "In the resurrection they neither marry nor are given in marriage but are like angels in heaven. And as for the resurrection of the dead, have you not read what was said to you by God, 'I am the God of Abraham, the God of Isaac, and the God of Jacob'? He is God not of the dead, but of the living." (Matthew 22:29–32)

You know neither the scriptures nor the power of God. The logic we might apply to questions of eternity is the logic woven not with earthly mathematics but with the wisdom of heaven—the scriptures and a glimpse of the power of God. The God of the living.

Jesus looks deeply at the context and the heart and truth of God as he ponders the questions that come before him.

There is one other story that I would like us to consider with the two stories we have been given in our Gospel reading: the story of the woman caught in adultery that we find in John 8. Jesus is approached by some religious leaders. "Teacher, this woman was caught in the very act of committing adultery. Now in the law Moses commanded us to stone such women. Now what do you say?" Again, the aim is to trap Jesus so that they might charge him. What he does is very beautiful. He doesn't rush into a decision. He kneels down and he writes with his finger in the sand. He ponders. And then he says, "Let anyone among you who is without sin be the first to throw a stone at her." And then, again, he bends down and writes in the sand. They think about this and then, one by one, they go away. It isn't that he doesn't acknowledge that this woman has done something wrong. He does. But he tells her he does not condemn her. And then he says to her, "Go your way, and from now on do not sin again." (John 8:1–11)

Three stories that show us Jesus pondering difficult questions. Exploring the context of the questions and the hearts of those who ask them. And the hearts of those involved. And the ways of God. Which is what I guess he would ask of us, as we ponder the questions that are asked of us, knowing he is with us. That we ponder the context. Take a coin and hold it and turn it over and see what it tells us. Resist the temptation to use logic that does not belong. Sit and draw in the sand and wonder. Never, never answer out of ignorance. The questions we are asked deserve to be explored as deeply as we can manage. And then our hearts. Oh, our hearts.

What would he ask us? Are you frightened when you ponder this question? Who would want you to be frightened? Are they worthy of your trust? God always says "Don't." Don't be frightened. Never allow fear to drive you, though I understand that it often does. I am with you so try not to be frightened.

Have you sinned? Before you judge another, have you sinned? Sit in the sand and look into my eyes and let us explore if you have sinned.

Do you understand? Have you thought and read and questioned and discussed, have you held coins and seen what they mean?

We hope we do our best when we are confronted with questions or struggles or situations in the world, which seem so full of violence and terror that we are shaken to our core and can barely think or hold a coin and ponder or sit in the sand . . . and he knows that.

He faced many occasions when they tried to trap him. He saw through them and the way he thought and the way he answered guides us. But they trapped him in the end. Ambushed him in a garden with the kiss of one who was his friend, and the denial of another, and a trial where he seems to stop guiding them anymore, a trial where he was . . . silent. They trapped him in the end. Pinned him down to die on a cross. And it looked as if those who would trap him had won.

Only two mornings later he was there asking his questions, looking into their hearts, again. "Why are you crying?" he said to Mary. "What are you discussing on the road?" he said to the two disciples walking to Emmaus. "Do you love me?" To Peter, of course . . . and to all of us. Two mornings after they thought they had finally caught him, he ambushed them with love and life. He might have been turning over coins in his hand or writing in the sand. He showed them his hands and his side and the wounds of the violence there. And broke bread and fed them and forgave them and sent them out. Two mornings later he was the one asking questions as he ambushed them with love and life.

He's there with us the morning after too. The morning after we answer questions, whatever questions are put before us. For some the grief of the answers is hard to bear and new questions must be found. Again, we turn to him to help us answer them.

Sometimes, though, the situation is too dire for questions. There is such violence. Such terror. Such disbelief. Such grief. As we have witnessed in recent days in Israel and in Gaza.

He's there. There in the midst of the violence too. He has no time there to look at coins or even to draw lines in the sand. No time for questions. They must come later. For now, he is holding a dying Israeli child cradled in one arm and a dying Palestinian child cradled in the other arm, and there are tears pouring down his cheeks.

CHAPTER 33

Allowing God to be God

As we gather on this Third Sunday in the Season of Lent, we find ourselves invited to reflect on the idea of repentance. Lent is a time when we are encouraged to spend a little time reflecting, perhaps on the blessings of our lives, perhaps on our frailties, perhaps on the suffering of those we love or those living in places of war, perhaps on those things of which we are ashamed. Sin, to use a theological word. The Jesuit writer Gerard Hughes said that "Sin is the failure to let God be God." Perhaps repentance is a step in the direction of allowing God to be God. Perhaps it is a step in the direction of allowing *us* to be most fully *us*.

It is interesting that the image used for those in need of repentance, in the reading from the prophet Isaiah, and in this morning's psalm, is of ones who are *thirsty*. It is interesting also, that the image of the one who accompanies our repentance, who hears our confessions and forgives our sins, the image of God, is of an abundance of *water*.

The prophet Isaiah bids us reflect on these things with these words:

> Ho, everyone who thirsts,
>   come to the waters; . . .
> Seek the Lord while he may be found,
>   call upon him while he is near;
> let the wicked forsake their way,
>   and the unrighteous their thoughts;
> let them return to the Lord, that he may have mercy on them,
>   and to our God, for he will abundantly pardon. (Isaiah 55:1,6–7)

In Psalm 63, the psalmist continues the theme:

> O God, you are my God, I seek you,
> my soul thirsts for you;
> my flesh faints for you,
> as in a dry and weary land where there is no water. (Psalm 63:1)

The prophets, the psalmists, and most especially Jesus, use images from the natural world to give us insight into the ways of life in God, the ways of being human, and of the nature of God. Sometimes those images resonate for us and help us see what we might not have seen before. Oh . . . yes . . . we can be like that, we might think as we hear a verse or two of scripture. Oh . . . I wonder if God might be like that . . . when we hear a verse or two more. It is also true that, at times, images fail.

Living in our country we know what it is to lack water. We may have travelled or lived in parts of Australia where water is scarce and to know the great blessing when water comes. These images might well give insight to the blessing of God's presence and the struggle when God seems absent. Just at the moment, we know well that there are parts of our nation where floods are wreaking so much damage that if we invited those who live there to see God as an abundance of water, we would cause them to laugh if the matter was not so serious. Images do at times fail.

Jesus is the master of using stories and images to help us see the truth that he longs that we might know. Of the presence of the one who he knows as Abba, Father, of the reality of sin and struggle, of the longing of God to forgive and set free.

We come across Jesus, in our reading from Luke 13, in conversation with a crowd. This crowd is reflecting on the local news—just as we might—news about those who are suffering. Not unlike the well-known friends of Job, who assumed that his sufferings must have been caused by some sin he had committed, members of this crowd want Jesus to reassure them that the people who are suffering must have done something wrong:

> This crowd told Jesus about the Galileans whose blood Pilate had mingled with their sacrifices. He asked them, "Do you think that because these Galileans suffered in this way they were worse sinners than all other Galileans? No, I tell you; but unless you repent, you will all perish as they did. Or those eighteen who were

> killed when the tower of Siloam fell on them—do you think that they were worse offenders than all the others living in Jerusalem? No, I tell you; but unless you repent, you will all perish just as they did." (Luke 13:1–5)

The first story is about some Galileans who have been murdered, the second about a group of people who died when a building fell upon them. Jesus is blunt, "No I tell you," he says. Anyone might die in this way.

Not unlike members of this crowd, we find ourselves listening to news stories about those who suffer. These last weeks our hearts and minds, our prayers, have grieved for the people of Ukraine and the people of Russia. Did we hear the story of the bombing of a maternity hospital? Did we hear just days ago that the woman, soon to give birth, that we saw carried on a stretcher from the rubble, died a few days later, her baby dying with her? Did we see the woman of Russian and Ukrainian descent who interrupted the main news programme on Russia's state TV Channel One, holding up a sign behind the studio presenter with slogans denouncing the war in Ukraine? Protester Marina Ovsyannikova was arrested after denouncing war on live Russian television. We can only dread the suffering that will be meted out on this extraordinarily courageous woman. It is unlikely we would question Jesus about any guilt in these stories. It is unlikely he would need to say . . . "No, I tell you . . ."

His words "unless you repent" might haunt us a little. What does he mean? How does he say these words? Kindly or fiercely? After these words, he says a little more . . . but it's a parable, isn't it? Do we dare wonder about the parable he tells?

The parable is about a fruit tree, a tree that grows figs, in fact (Luke 13:6–9). Only this one doesn't. The owner of the vineyard comes to collect some figs and on finding the tree bare he calls the gardener. "See here!" the owner of the vineyard says. "For three years I have come looking for fruit on this fig tree, and still, I find none. Cut it down! Why should it be wasting the soil?"

Do we relate to this sometimes? Do we sometimes feel that whatever we are meant for isn't bearing fruit? For us, or our community, or our nation, or even the whole planet? Do we sometimes feel that our vocation is not bearing fruit? According to the owner of the vineyard it is the tree's fault. Do we resonate with this? That we are made to thrive in some way, and that we are not, and that it is our fault?

Scripture always sheds light on who we are, we human beings, and on who God is. Do we imagine God looking at us as the vineyard owner looks at the tree? With disappointment, in judgement, deciding to give up? Do we imagine God looking at us like that?

There's another character in this parable, did we notice? There is the gardener. He speaks on behalf of the tree, the fruitless tree. "Sir," he says to the vineyard owner, "let it alone for one more year, until I dig round it and put manure on it. If it bears fruit next year, well and good; but if not, you can cut it down." Is it possible that the vineyard owner, the disappointed one, the one who gives up, is more like us? Would we give up, on ourselves or on one another? Would we cut down the fig tree and throw it away?

Is it possible that God is the gardener? The one kneeling on the ground with hands covered in soil, and a trowel ready to dig around the tree and put manure on it? Is it possible that God is the gardener?

We might ponder this—who God is like for us? Whether our image of God is of one who judges, perhaps sensibly, but firmly, giving up on those who do not perform. Or is our image of God like the gardener, pleading for a second chance for us, longing that he might nurture us into life? Perhaps pouring water on the thirsty tree, if we remember the images from Isaiah and the psalm.

As we ponder this Lent the idea of making our confession, of repenting, of turning towards God, part of our reflection might be on what God looks like for us. Whether, perhaps, God is like the gardener, who only wanted another chance for the struggling tree. Perhaps we might turn towards God who is a little like that as we ponder the things of which we are ashamed in this holy Season of Lent.

CHAPTER 34

Standing under a waterfall

They are some of the most well-known words in scripture, the words Jesus spoke to Nicodemus that night:

> For God so loved the world that he gave his only Son, so that everyone who believes in him may not perish but may have eternal life. (John 3:16)

The story is told in the third chapter of John's Gospel. Nicodemus, a religious leader, has sensed from the things that Jesus is doing that he is from God, but Nicodemus is wondering how this can be. In John's Gospel, where light and dark are such powerful symbols, it matters that Nicodemus comes to Jesus by night. The idea is that he doesn't understand. The Gospel passage that we have heard read this morning is a strange one really, a snippet of a conversation between Jesus and Nicodemus, coming after the part where Jesus speaks about being born again and Nicodemus has no idea what he is talking about. Nicodemus is thinking in earthly terms, in physical terms. But Jesus is not talking about the physical life. He is talking about the spiritual life. He tries to explain this:

> No one can enter the kingdom of God without being born of water and Spirit. What is born of the flesh is flesh, and what is born of the Spirit is spirit. Do not be astonished that I said to you, "You must be born from above." (John 3:5–6)

Jesus has come from above. From the heart of the life of God.

He tries to explain this to Nicodemus, referring to himself as the Son of Man, what one spiritual thinker called "the emblem of our humanity", the ultimate human being who is at home in earth as he is in heaven.

"No one has ascended into heaven except the one who descended from heaven, the Son of Man," Jesus keeps trying to explain. "And just as Moses lifted up the serpent in the wilderness, so must the Son of Man be lifted up, that whoever believes in him may have eternal life." (John 3:13–15)

Nicodemus could be excused for being even more confused now. Jesus is referring to the Old Testament story that we heard read this morning. Travelling in the wilderness, the people led by Moses find themselves being attacked by poisonous serpents. God tells Moses to make a serpent of bronze and put it upon a pole; and whenever a serpent bites someone, that person is to look at the serpent of bronze and live (Numbers 21:9).

This is a very strange story. But there is something significant going on in it, and it's worth thinking about it as Jesus is relating it to his being lifted up to his death on the cross.

God is, in the bronze serpent, in some sense inhabiting the deaths inflicted by the serpents. God is in solidarity with us when illness strikes. If the person who is bitten has the faith to look up, to look up at the serpent of bronze, healing will come. This is again about the spiritual life, about the praying life, about the people in the wilderness being encouraged to have faith in the context of illness and death. It's about God being present there, bringing life there.

Jesus is inviting Nicodemus and all of us into Life, the spiritual life, eternal life:

> For God so loved the world that he gave his only Son, so that everyone who believes in him may not perish but may have eternal life.

When I was at theological college, our New Testament lecturer translated this verse from John's Gospel in a way that surprised me, and so I have not forgotten her words. She said that the writer is not having Jesus say that God loved the world *so* much that he gave his son. The writer is saying something else entirely. The writer is saying that God loved the world "so" . . . *in this way. This is the way* in which God loved the world.

God longed to be known by us. Longs to be known by us. How best might God do this, might God be known? The best way for a human being to know God is through a human being. One who is so close to God, one who links earth and heaven, one who walks the earth and stands alongside the human beings in his time and place in all the aspects of their lives. One who eats meals with us and teaches us. One who keeps company with frail and broken bodies, with troubled minds and spirits. One who inhabits the thing so many most dread, death and the fear of the meaningless that we might think death brings. Jesus even dies with us, is lifted up on the cross—the Son of Man is lifted up, that whoever believes in him may have eternal life.

God loved the world *so* . . . in this way. The Word became flesh and dwelt among us, as the prologue to John's Gospel says. God gave us Jesus, that believing in him we might have life, eternal life.

So, we might reflect on that, on those words, eternal life. Being like Nicodemus, the one who comes at night, remember, we are prone to think in the realm of space and time, of what we can see, of what we can measure. Eternal life is not about time going on, though. It is not about endless life. It is about something different entirely. Rowan Williams in our Lent Book *Candles in the Dark*, put it this way:

> Our identity as Christians is to be in the place where Jesus stands, the place from which we see into the boundless reality that is the outpouring of God's life. Standing with Jesus, standing in the truth, is like standing under a waterfall: the life of God is around us, soaking and overwhelming us. We can't grab it and hold on to it, we can't contain it. The mystery of the Trinitarian life . . . is the mystery of just being immersed in this.[1]

Standing with Jesus, standing in the truth is like standing under a waterfall. The life of God around us, soaking and overwhelming us.

---

1 Rowan Williams, *Candles in the Dark: Faith, Hope and Love in a Time of Pandemic* (London: SPCK, 2020), p. 33.

I wonder how that resonates with us. For each one of us it will be different. We may have sensed this, this waterfall, or eternal life may have been almost like a whisper, something we have only just sensed, barely known, glimpsed in the distance. What do the words "eternal life" mean to us?

Today is the Fourth Sunday in Lent, Mothering Sunday. Traditionally it was a time for those who had moved away from home to return home; to return to their family home or their family church. It's a time to return to their roots, as the saying goes. Mothering Sunday might be just the time to ponder what eternal life might mean for us. It is a time of refreshment from our Lenten disciplines. A time for remembering, wondering, what the word "home" means to us. A time to pause and reflect. Where were we most nurtured, where did we first glimpse the possibility of eternal life? Or where did we sense God's presence? Love's presence? The presence of forgiveness? With whom? A person, our family, a faith community? It might have been our school, or the group of people with whom we sang in a choir or played a most loved sport. It might have been in a book, in the words of a spiritual writer, or a wise novelist. Where were we at home? Where *are* we most at home? Eternal life has something to do with this place. On Mothering Sunday, we might ponder this.

This day is one on which we are encouraged to pause before we turn again and walk the final weeks of Lent, the days of Holy Week . . . before we face the sharp darkness of Good Friday, the day on which Jesus, the Son of Man, is lifted up, dies a criminal's death, that we might have this precious thing, eternal life. Believing in him, we may have eternal life.

The one who wrote John's Gospel said that he did so that we might believe, and through believing have life. I don't think it's about some fierce intellectual effort, this believing. It's not about understanding a set of complex ideas. Belief may well be woven with doubt. Belief may well ebb and flow. Belief may be the clearest thing one day and yet a complete mystery on another. The thing is, we are not alone in it. This Son of Man, this Jesus, accompanies us in it, as we accompany one another. It may be that it is just possible that we will notice that . . . "standing with Jesus, standing in the truth, is like standing under a waterfall: the life of God is around us, soaking and overwhelming us".[2]

---

2 Williams, *Candles in the Dark*, p. 33.

CHAPTER 35

Known by name

A story is told of a Jewish Rabbi Zusya. When Rabbi Zusya grew old and knew that his time on earth was nearing a close, his students gathered around him. One of them asked if he was afraid of dying.

"I am afraid of what God will ask me," the Rabbi said.

"What will he ask you?"

"He will not ask me, 'Zusya, why were you not like Moses?' He will ask me, 'Zusya, why were you not like Zusya?'"

He will ask me, "Zusya, why were you not like Zusya?"[1]

God names us, calls us by name, gives us our identity, the essence of who we are . . . for we are vocation bearers and our vocations, unique to each one of us, are always about bringing life in some part of the world.

We arrive in the cathedral on this the Fourth Sunday of Easter with the stories of Jesus' resurrection ringing in our ears. For the first three Sundays of Easter, we have seen Jesus encounter his grief-stricken and troubled disciples, speaking their names and meeting them in their place of need. When he speaks their names he reminds them of their identity; when he meets them in their place of need, he addresses wherever it is that their vocation struggles to thrive.

Mary was grief stricken. "Why are you weeping?" ask the angels in the tomb, and Jesus who she thought to be a gardener. Jesus spoke Mary's name and she spoke his name for her, "Rabbouni, teacher". Jesus healed Mary's sorrow and sent her into the world to be Mary, to tell the news that he was alive.

---

1 Quoted in John Shea, *The Relentless Widow* (Collegeville, MN: Liturgical Press, 2006), p. 134.

On the Second Sunday of Easter, we saw Jesus encounter Thomas. Thomas was not present when Jesus appeared to the other disciples, speaking his words of peace. Thomas refused to believe unless he could see Jesus' wounds and place his fingers in them. And, so, Jesus gave him what he needed. Presence, his physical presence, and Thomas believed. "My Lord and my God," he said. Again, Jesus is named. Jesus spoke of us in this encounter with Thomas, of those who cannot physically see him, cannot gaze in awe at his wounds. He called us blessed. "Blessed are those who have not seen and yet have believed." As if he knows that on some days doubt, like Thomas' doubt, is so very real. He knows that belief and trust are not easy.

Then there was Peter. We know that Peter was weighed down with guilt. Beside the charcoal fire, Jesus forgave Peter's threefold denial and gave him his vocation, to be the one who would feed God's sheep, to be the one to lead Jesus' church in the world.

Which brings us to this Sunday and the theme of sheep. We might expect, on this Fourth Sunday of Easter, to hear another resurrection story, perhaps about the two disciples on the road to Emmaus, but we find ourselves, instead, in the tenth chapter of John's Gospel, where Jesus helps us ponder *our own relationship* with the risen Christ. How does Jesus encounter us? It is true that we might well reflect on the resurrection accounts, imagine ourselves in the scenes and find there Jesus speaking our names, healing our guilts, tending to our doubts. Jesus also reaches us through images found in nature and, in John's Gospel, Jesus links the words "I am", the God words of the Old Testament, to images with which those around him could relate: water, bread, a vine. Today it is the image of a shepherd and that shepherd's relationship with the sheep he tends. He wants us to feel, to know, to imagine what God is like for us, for those of us who cannot actually see the risen Christ, and so he appeals to our imaginations.

In verses just before those of our Gospel reading Jesus says, "I am the Good Shepherd." The shepherd calls his own sheep by name and leads them out. When he has brought out all his own, he goes ahead of them, and the sheep follow him because they know his voice.

How will Jesus meet us? How will he tend to our struggles, our frailties, our sins? Jesus appeals to our imaginations, giving us the image of a shepherd. "I am the Good Shepherd," he says. This shepherd knows our names, knows our identities, knows our deepest needs. Jesus, exploring this image further, speaks of us. This shepherd's sheep hear his voice.

David F. Ford is a Cambridge theologian who has been working for the last 20 years on a commentary on John's Gospel. He calls it a theological commentary. I heard him speaking with Justin Welby, the Archbishop of Canterbury, on a Facebook video, as it happens. It was a short conversation, but in it one sensed a man of very interesting ideas and so I ordered a copy of his book. In coming months, David Ford will be our guide at times, especially when the text is from the Gospel of John.

In his introduction, he explores the idea that there are three key themes in John's Gospel. He writes that the leading question running through the whole Gospel is "Who is Jesus?" The second key theme is that Jesus' Spirit is given without measure to us for the ongoing drama of loving. The third theme is about God's love for all creation. The first question that Jesus asks his disciples in John's Gospel is "What are you looking for?"[2]

The Gospel is about identity, about our names. It's about Jesus' identity and our own. Who is this Jesus? And what are we looking for? When the resurrection of Jesus breaks into creation we see in the Gospel stories the effect on those who loved Jesus, Mary, Thomas, Peter, the disciples on the Road to Emmaus. The question for us is: what is the effect of Jesus' resurrection on us?

David Ford writes this about the resurrection:

> All the post resurrection encounters were surprises, and they were not obvious or straightforward. There is no reason to think that recognizing the free self-revelations of Jesus now will be any less challenging and surprising, or that either the current followers of Jesus or anyone else, will be able to anticipate to whom or how they will be granted.[3]

---

2 David F. Ford, *The Gospel of John: A Theological Commentary* (Grand Rapids, MI: Baker Academic, 2021), pp. 4–10.

3 Ford, *The Gospel of John: A Theological Commentary*, p. 13.

> The resurrection of Jesus cannot be understood simply as a historical event alongside others such as his crucifixion . . . it is a "God-sized" event in which God acts.[4]

Can we imagine being encountered by a God-sized event in which God acts, an utterly surprising encounter?

The image of Jesus as shepherd and of us as sheep might help as we wonder about this. We are so accustomed to speaking ourselves, to acting, controlling, enabling things to happen. It is difficult not to wonder what we might need to do to set the stage for such an encounter with God. The image of shepherd and the sheep seems to invite us to think a little differently about this. The shepherd is the one who leads and speaks. The sheep in turn follow and listen and hear the shepherd's voice. What is being asked of us is a gentle thing, a vulnerable thing, a way of being that allows for the presence of a shepherd, of one who is utterly to be trusted, of one who gives eternal life, and from whose hand we will never be taken, in whose presence we are utterly safe.

The shepherd speaks our names and we are to hear his voice. We might do well to sit in silence, perhaps, to pray without words, to allow our cathedral building, or the music of the choir, or the waves of the sea to calm us. Listening is our vocation in this, silence, stillness, is our stance, it seems. Then, quietly, almost silently, we hear Jesus speaking our names, and we may know a little more clearly who God is calling us to be.

When Rabbi Zusya grew old and knew that his time on earth was nearing a close, his students gathered around him. One of them asked if he was afraid of dying.

"I am afraid of what God will ask me," the Rabbi said.

"What will he ask you?"

"He will not ask me, 'Zusya, why were you not like Moses?' He will ask me, 'Zusya, why were you not like Zusya?'"

He will ask me, "Zusya, why were you not like Zusya?"

Zusya, do you see, was his name.

---

4 Ford, *The Gospel of John: A Theological Commentary*, p. 14.

CHAPTER 36

Thriving in God

> I am the true vine, and my Father is the vine-grower. . . . I am the vine, you are the branches. (John 15:1,5)

This morning's Gospel reading is from the Gospel of John, that Gospel heavily woven with theology, with words about who God is, who Jesus is, and who we are in relationship with God. The Gospel opens with the most beautiful poetry set before the dawn of time . . . "In the beginning was the Word, and the Word was with God, and the Word was God. He was in the beginning with God." As the poetry of the prologue unfolds, the incarnation is pronounced. "And the Word became flesh and dwelt among us, . . . full of grace and truth" (John 1:1,2,14).

As the story of Jesus' earthly life, this dwelling among us, unfolds in this Gospel of John, insight into Jesus' identity is found in the *signs* he performs and in the *words* he speaks. Today we hear one of the seven sets of words spoken by Jesus that begin with the words "I am".

The words *I am the true vine* are taken from John 15. Jesus has just gathered with his disciples at the last supper, he has just washed the disciples' feet. He has given them his new commandment about love. Then he begins to speak with them at length. At the supper table, he says the words, "Do not let your hearts be troubled" that we often hear read at funerals, and at the end of this time of speaking Jesus says, "Rise, let us be on our way." Just before the words we read this morning, Jesus says, "Rise, let us be on our way" (John 14:1,31).

Jesus and the disciples are walking now. They are walking on their way to Gethsemane, the garden where Jesus will cry out to his Father in fear and grief and the garden where Judas' betrayal will come to light. Let us imagine them walking. As they walk, Jesus continues to explain, to describe, to help the disciples understand what they mean to him, who he is for them, and his closeness with his Father.

And he uses the words "I am". *Ego eimi* in the Greek, "I am".

You probably know what I am about to say, just as the disciples would have immediately thought of what I am about to say. This matters. Jesus is using all the literary, theological words and stories in his power to reach them, to reach us. We will think about that in a little while. *His longing* that they glimpse the truth of who he is and who they are in relationship with him. *His longing* that we glimpse the truth of who he is and who we are in relationship with him.

You and they know what I am about to say. It's about the Exodus story, about that foundational story of the Jewish faith. It's about the Israelites in slavery and God longing to set them free; God calling Moses and asking him to help bring the Israelites out of Egypt and into the Promised Land. It's about Moses saying to God who was speaking out of that bush that was burning, "Who shall I say sent me?" and about God's reply, "I am who I am." "I am who I am." These are the God words. There is no doubt here that Jesus is using the God words. No doubt that shivers would have gone down the spines of the Jewish disciples as they heard what he said and knew what he meant. This is God we are talking about here.

The Dean of Canterbury Cathedral, Robert Willis, also longs that people know the love of God and the presence of God during this pandemic time where, for long periods of time, many people in England and across the world have been in lockdown. Where so many have been unable to spend much time worshipping with others and enjoying time out in nature. For over a year now, every day, Dean Robert has prayed Morning Prayer in his Deanery garden, with what he calls his online "Garden Congregation". The half-hour times of prayer involve prayers, psalms, readings and remembrances of anniversaries of births and deaths. Woven into these prayers are profound reflections on themes that emerge. A few weeks ago, Dean Robert reflected on the "I am" sayings from the Gospel of John, and this is what he said about the words "I am":

> Jesus is saying, focus on me . . . in the present tense . . . nothing is more present than the verb "to be" and nothing more intimate than the verb "to be" in the first person singular—in English "I

> am", in the Greek *ego eimi* . . . this takes us back to Moses with the fire of the burning bush and saying to God . . . who shall I say sent me . . . and the words "I am" take us all the way back . . . takes us not only to the centre of ourselves when we say it, not even to the centre of the human Jesus, but to the centre of all created things and beyond . . . it's in that that we have the capacity to reach out for our humanity and to know that life that has no end.[1]

Jesus is saying, focus on me . . . in the present tense . . . nothing is more present than the verb "to be" and nothing more intimate than the verb "to be".

These words are about closeness with Jesus . . . it's "in that, that we have the capacity to reach out for our humanity and to know that life that has no end".

As Jesus and his disciples make their solemn walk to the Garden of Gethsemane, he uses the image of the vine. He names himself the true vine and his father the vine grower and we, we are the branches. The image of the vine was very significant in Jewish theology. The people of God were often referred to as a vine. When the people of God let God down the prophet Isaiah spoke of God the planter expecting grapes, but the vine yielded only wild grapes (Isaiah 5:1–7).

Using this image of the vine, Jesus gives it new meaning. As one writer puts it:

> Jesus's [identity] is lodged in the context of his relationship with God and . . . of his relationship with the community of his followers. . . . All three elements—gardener, vine and branches—are essential to the production of fruit . . . Jesus [is] the middle ground between God and the community.[2]

---

1 Dean Robert Willis, Canterbury Cathedral Morning Prayer, Wednesday 14 April 2020.

2 Gail R. O'Day, *The Gospel of John*, New Interpreter's Bible (Nashville, TN: Abingdon Press, 1995), p. 757.

Then, to highlight the relationships he is describing, Jesus uses a beautiful word, the word "abide":

> Abide in me as I abide in you. Just as the branch cannot bear fruit by itself unless it abides in the vine, neither can you unless you abide in me. (John 15:4)

Vines and the fruit that grows on them are not strange for us, either. Vineyards adorn our state and visiting them is one of the joys of those of us who live here and visitors alike. So, the image of the vine, with its trunk and roots in the earth and the image of the branches, utterly dependent on that vine, and the image of the ones who tend that vine are images on which we can ponder. Cedar Prest, who created the stained-glass clerestory windows in the nave of our cathedral, was inspired by Jesus' words and the northern windows in particular are rich with the vines and vineyards that are characteristic of so many different areas of the South Australian settlement.

I guess what Jesus wants us to know is, firstly, our dependence on the vine. There is simply no life for the branch without the vine and without the gardener who tends and prunes. I think that Jesus would also want us to know that the thriving of the branches comes from the vine, from the care of the gardener.

As Dean Robert put it:

> the words "I am" take us all the way back. . . . take us not only to the centre of ourselves when we say it, not even to the centre of the human Jesus, but to the centre of all created things and beyond . . . it's in that that we have the capacity to reach out for our humanity and to know that life that has no end.[3]

Thriving. That is what life in connection with God is about. Thriving. As Jesus walks with his disciples on the way to his trial and death, he is giving them images to hold on to, images to remember, so that when they

---

3 Dean Robert Willis, Canterbury Cathedral Morning Prayer, Wednesday, 14 April 2020.

are almost broken by what will happen, and when the resurrection in all its wonder and all its mystery comes, these images will nurture them, remind them, restore them. When we find ourselves walking, perhaps at a time of grief, or utter confusion, or awful doubt, these images might nurture us, remind us, restore us.

They remind us that we are as dependent on God who we know in Jesus as a branch is dependent on the vine, and that we thrive in God who we know in Jesus as a branch thrives in a vine. Jesus longs that we know this, even as he faced the most terrifying time of his life, loved his disciples so much that he spoke with such depth and care so that they would know that abiding in him is where they would thrive.

CHAPTER 37

Sitting in a ditch

How do we live a good life, as individuals, as a society? What does the Lord require of us? And how do we know if we are doing the right thing?

God, through the prophet Amos, speaks about a plumb-line:

> This is what he showed me: the LORD was standing beside a wall built with a plumb-line, with a plumb-line in his hand. And the LORD said to me, "Amos, what do you see?" And I said, "A plumb-line." Then the LORD said,
> "See, I am setting a plumb-line
> in the midst of my people Israel;
> I will never again pass them by;
> the high places of Isaac shall be made desolate,
> and the sanctuaries of Israel shall be laid waste,
> and I will rise against the house of Jeroboam
> with the sword." (Amos 7:7–9)

In the context of building and construction, the plumb-line tests if a building is upright. In the context of God and God's people at the time of the prophet Amos, the time of King Jeroboam II in the eighth century before Christ, the plumb-line is a test of justice and righteousness:

> But let justice roll down like waters
> And righteousness like an ever-flowing stream.

God cried out through the prophet. (Amos 5:24)

In a land and time when immense prosperity was based on the rich taking from the poor, the people of Israel failed the plumb-line test.

The lawyer in our reading this morning from Luke's Gospel would have known about Amos' plumb-line, known about God's longing for justice and righteousness. He would have known the scriptures well.

"What must I do to inherit eternal life?" this lawyer asks Jesus. It's a critical question, a life and death question. Jesus would approve of the question. He's here that we might have life, remember. Jesus points the lawyer, not to the prophets, but to the law. "What is written in the law? What do you read there?" Jesus says. The lawyer answers, "You shall love the Lord your God with all your heart, and with all your soul, and with all your strength, and with all your mind; and your neighbour as yourself." We could have answered Jesus' question ourselves. We know the most important commandments too (Luke 10:25–28).

But this lawyer wants things defined, he wants them clear. Perhaps he wants Jesus to give him a plumb-line. What he seems to want is a programme of action and clear guidelines on the limits of the action required. Who is my neighbour? Give me some boundaries. Limit the group of people for whom I must feel some responsibility. I want eternal life. But I want the way to this life to be achievable and measurable.

Jesus is not interested in definitions and guidelines and a boundary on compassion. He knows that God's kingdom doesn't work like this. So, he tells a story. We know this story very well. We talk about people being Good Samaritans. The trouble with knowing a story well is that it can stunt the liberating power of the story for us. We will need to find a new way of experiencing this story if it is going to transform us.

Like all good stories, this story begins with a problem:

> A man was going down from Jerusalem to Jericho, and fell into the hands of robbers, who stripped him, beat him, and went away, leaving him half dead. (Luke 10:30)

We know nothing about the man; he could be any of us. As we explore this story we will, in fact, find ourselves in the ditch with him. Those listening to the story would have known about the road on which the man walked. The road from Jerusalem to Jericho was notoriously dangerous. They would have *felt* the danger.

The next words in the story give hope: "By chance" this man is not the only one on the road. Like many stories, this story uses a series of three—three people pass by the beaten man, a priest, a Levite and a Samaritan. Those listening would have expected the third traveller to have been an ordinary man, an Israelite. Those listening would have expected the story to include someone who wasn't religious doing the right thing, being better observers of the law than the religious people. But the one who helps the beaten man is in fact an enemy of the Jewish people, the last person they would have expected to obey the law.

For us to be moved by this story, as those who were listening to Jesus would have been moved, we need to see it a little differently. The priest is someone deeply trusted to obey the law. The Levite is someone also trusted to do the right thing. For us to be shocked, as those listening to the story would have been shocked, we need to imagine two people we trust to care for us *walking past* the beaten man, and then a person that we view as utterly untrustworthy—perhaps someone who we find difficult, or someone who we find unreliable, or someone we find disturbing—seeing the man, stopping and offering care. With whom do we feel most uncomfortable? Who is a Samaritan for us?

What does the behaviour of the Samaritan look like? What did he do? The priest *saw* the beaten man and *passed by* on the other side. The Levite also *saw* the beaten man and *passed by* on the other side. The Samaritan also *saw* the beaten man. They all *saw* the man. But the Samaritan saw a *human being*. When he saw the man, he was moved with pity:

> He went to him and bandaged his wounds, having poured oil and wine on them. Then he put him on his own animal, brought him to an inn, and took care of him. (Luke 10:34)

He went, he bandaged, he poured oil and wine, he put him on his animal, he took him to the inn and took care of him there. This is what compassion looks like.

While the hearers of the story are reeling at the identity of the man who brings healing, the one beaten at the side of the road doesn't mind who helps him. What he needs is his compassion.

Having told the story, Jesus looks the lawyer in the eye and asks:

> Which of these three, do you think, was a neighbour to the man who fell into the hands of the robbers? (Luke 10:36)

The lawyer cannot bring himself to use the word Samaritan, we notice. The neighbour is "The one who showed the beaten man mercy". "Go and do likewise," Jesus says (Luke 10:37).

All of a sudden, the lawyer finds himself in the ditch with the beaten man. The lawyer had asked Jesus to define neighbour, to give limits on those to whom he should offer the love referred to in the law. But Jesus has twisted the question around. We are looking at the question now from the point of view of the one who is beaten by the side of the road. Three people have seen this man. Who has been a neighbour to him? Who has been moved with pity, who has responded with godly compassion? The question is not about who we should help, it is about the essence of the quality of a neighbour. Jesus has shown the vocation of neighbour in his story.

The lawyer asked for boundaries and not only has Jesus refused to put boundaries on who is neighbour and so also who is not neighbour, he has broken down the boundaries about who belongs in the fold of the children of God. The Samaritan, who definitely did not belong, is, in the story, the one who enacts the love of God, the one who knows and enacts the two most fundamental commandments in the Jewish Law.

The lawyer's question has been superseded by a more fundamental question about neighbourliness in the kingdom of God. As one scholar put it, "One cannot define one's neighbour; one can only be a neighbour."[1]

A lawyer comes up to Jesus and asks a question, a very important question about eternal life. Jesus answers him with a story. The temptation for us is to do with the story what the lawyer tried to do with the commandments; to extract from the story a definition or two, a programme of action, some clear guidelines on the limits of the action required. Only that is not what stories are for. Stories are like seeds planted in the ground, planted in our hearts, perhaps, disturbing us, causing us to wonder, leaving us a little unsure, and yet . . . leaving us with

---

1 Quoted in Arland J. Hultgren, *The Parables of Jesus* (Grand Rapids, MI: Eerdmans Publishing, 2000), p. 99.

a sense that there is a deep truth there that we have not quite grasped but that it is well worth our while sitting with for a time.

The scholar Walter Brueggemann said that "people are not changed by ethical urging but by transformed imagination".[2] He might have said we are not changed by definitions and programmes of action but by stories that disturb and puzzle us. I sometimes think that Jesus' parables are like the grains of sand that irritate an oyster until a pearl is formed. Somehow, we need to let them irritate.

We end up like the man in the ditch, really, as we struggle to understand the spiritual life, and the ethical life, and the day-to-day life of trying to do the right thing.

Who walks by?

There'll be those who give us definitions and plans of action. There'll be those who tell us what is wrong with us, leaving us feeling guilty.

And then a man might walk by. The one who will feed us at this Eucharist.

This man called Jesus, who sees us, sees the struggle of it all, sees the longing for definitions and simple answers, sees the guilt that can constrict us when we wonder what it is that God requires of us and we know that we have so often failed. He sees it all; and he sits down beside us and binds up our wounds and then . . . tells us a story. We don't really get the story. In many ways, it puzzles us. Somehow, though, we know that the answer to the lawyer's question, our question, how is it that we inherit eternal life, somehow the answer to this question will never be straightforward and might just be found in the story of the one who keeps us company in a ditch on the side of a road.

---

2 Walter Brueggemann, *Hopeful Imagination* (Philadelphia: Fortress Press, 1986), p. 25.

CHAPTER 38

All are welcome

Jesus just wants to heal the man standing in front of him with dropsy, a serious, life-threatening condition. They are at a meal, a significant social occasion, at the home of a prominent religious leader, not a social event to be interrupted and especially on the sabbath. These prominent leaders are watching him. He knows what's in their minds.

Jesus asks the legal question, appealing to those minds. "Is it lawful to cure people on the sabbath or not?" They are silent. So, Jesus heals the man and sends him away, away to live his life now, to thrive now. The ones in need of deep healing, though, are still before him at the meal. Their minds have failed them. So, Jesus appeals to their hearts. Stories reach the heart. "If one of you has a child or an ox that has fallen into a well, would you not immediately pull it out on a sabbath day?" he asks them (Luke 14:1–6). If we allow the story to reach us, can we feel the panic . . . a child in a well? Can we feel the urge to act immediately? What Jesus wants these religious leaders to know is that this is how it is for God when God's beloved ones are trapped in disease. It is *this* urgent. The longing to heal is *this* strong.

Jesus looks at those so in need of healing and he notices how they try to sit at the best places at the table. So, he tells them a parable. Remember, parables are subversive. We need to be careful with them. In them the ways of God and the nature of human beings are to be found. The questions we might ask of a parable could be: "What doesn't make sense? What is annoying me?"

> When you are invited by someone to a wedding banquet, [Jesus says] do not sit down at the place of honour, in case someone more distinguished than you has been invited by your host; and

> the host who invited both of you may come and say to you, "Give this person your place", and then in disgrace you would start to take the lowest place. But when you are invited, go and sit down at the lowest place, so that when your host comes, he may say to you, "Friend, move up higher"; then you will be honoured in the presence of all who sit at the table with you. (Luke 14:8–10)

Remember how we felt when we heard about the child in the well. The discomfort of it. Is there anything uncomfortable about this parable? Anything we don't get? Sit at the lowest place so you will be moved to the higher place? Really? Long for position but be more subtle about it? Manipulate the host to get what you want by appearing to be humble?

Is Jesus telling us this is how we might behave?

This is a parable, so we must expect to be puzzled. I think he's teasing us, telling us a joke, waiting to see if we get it. We might, at first, be hooked in by this story but if we sit with it for a moment we will see. See what we can be like. See how we long to sit in the place of significance. See our longing for significance. See that at times we would do anything to sit in the place of honour and feel honoured by all who are present.

If we sit with this for a time and notice . . . what will we then see? Him smiling at us. Yes, you are like that, aren't you? Yes, you do long to know you matter and you will at times do pretty well anything to be given that approval.

Does his heart break, for he knows how much we are approved of . . . how much we are loved? Does his heart break because we know so little?

What matters is that we have been invited to the banquet. That we belong. God longs for us to be there. I wonder about the table in God's kingdom, I wonder if the table in God's kingdom might not be *round*. I wonder if there is no higher place or lower place, there is just *a place*, and that place has our *name* on it. In the midst of places for all the others who God has created and who God loves, with their names on them. I wonder if at this round table in the kingdom of God, there is no place nearer or farther from the host's place, God's place, for the host is not sitting at the table. I wonder if it is not the truth that the host, God, is the one who serves at the table, the round table in the kingdom of God, where all are welcome.

It is not that God doesn't have requirements of us. God has given us the words of the law and the prophets to help us live well. God has given us the words and the stories and the presence, through the Holy Spirit, of Jesus to guide us and heal us and inspire us as we seek to live as God's children. God grieves when we move so far from understanding.

The prophets often speak for God, express God's voice.

The prophet Jeremiah, in our Old Testament reading this morning, says this:

> They have forsaken me,
> the fountain of living water,
> and dug out cisterns for themselves,
> cracked cisterns
> that can hold no water. (Jeremiah 2:13)

Feel the grief in that. God, the fountain of living water, knows that we have chosen for our god cracked cisterns that can hold no water.

For it is not that there isn't sin. The Jesuit writer Gerard Hughes says that "sin is the failure to let God be God". I found myself thinking about this, wondering what it is that God requires of us. I found myself thinking that we are made in the image of God. So, to let God be God is to allow ourselves to look like God, to live in that image of God. As we wonder what sin looks like, we might need to ask ourselves what God looks like. What God looks like, so that we might live as ones who bear God's image.

We know that God is love. One image for God is of the Trinity: God in three persons bound in loving relationship. Another important thing we read in the scriptures is that God is a God who made covenants with God's people. A covenant is a loyal loving relationship. The covenant that God makes with God's people is about God promising to stay in faithful relationship with God's people, whatever lies ahead. In Jeremiah 31 are the lovely words of the new covenant. God is speaking:

> I will put my law within them, and I will write it on their hearts; and I will be their God, and they shall be my people. No longer shall they teach one another, or say to each other, "Know the LORD", for they shall all know me, from the least of them to the

> greatest, says the LORD; for I will forgive their iniquity, and remember their sin no more. (Jeremiah 31:33–34)

What God is describing through the prophet Jeremiah is a relationship of faithful loving, of fidelity, of integrity. Is that the heart of the nature of God, perhaps? God is faithful love. Is this what God asks of us, perhaps? That being made in God's image, we love faithfully. Jesus says that the greatest commandments are that we love God and love our neighbour, that we are to love as God loves, with loyalty, with commitment. Is this what the one who is the fountain of living water longs for us?

Living in the image of the God who is love, we open our cathedral doors to gather in all who approach, just as God gathers in all who approach, gathers in all to sit at that round banquet table in the kingdom, in the parable Jesus told. Here all are welcome, here each has a place, a place on which is written their name.

Dates and texts of sermons

1. He was standing in the sea
Psalm 93; John 18:33–37
Preached on 21 November 2021

2. Succumbing to merciless physics
Isaiah 65:17–25; Luke 21:5–19
Preached on 17 November 2019

3. Poetry from two indigenous women
Mark 9:38–50
Preached on 26 September 2021

4. God's handiwork
Exodus 20:1–20; Matthew 21:33–46
Preached on 4 October 2020

5. About faith
Psalm 121
Preached on 20 October 2019

6. Under the wings of God
Psalm 91:1–6,14–16; Luke 16:19–31
Preached on 25 September 2022

7. A caress of God
Exodus 14:19–31
Preached on 13 September 2020

8. The first Sunday in lockdown—A man called Jesus
John 9:1–41

Preached on 22 March 2020

9. Prayer takes courage
John 14:15–21
Preached on 17 May 2020

10. We are not alone
1 Kings 10:1–13
Preached on 22 August 2021

11. What is God like?
Exodus 1:9—2:10; Matthew 16:13–20
Preached on 23 August 2020

12. An extraordinary truth
John 20:1–18
Preached on Easter Day 2021

13. God is always arriving
Isaiah 64:1–9; Mark 13:24–37
Preached on Advent Sunday 2020

14. Thin places
John 16:16–24
Preached on 16 May 2021

15. Revolution not comfort
Preached on 14 August 2022 for the Feast of Mary, Mother of Our Lord

16. Reflections on a grey puddle beside a cathedral
Preached on 27 June 2021 for the Feast of Saint Peter

17. Blindness
Luke 6:39–49
Preached on 27 February 2022

18. Nothing can be loved at speed
Isaiah 60:1–6; Matthew 2:1–12
Preached on the Feast of the Epiphany 2023

19. Awash with psalms
Psalm 51
Preached at Evensong on the First Sunday in Lent 2020

20. Love and fear
Mark 4:35–41
Preached on 20 June 2021

21. At a time of exile
Zephaniah 3:14–17; Philippians 4:4–7; Luke 3:7–18
Preached on 12 December 2021

22. Remembering of war
Preached on 13 November 2022 for Remembrance Sunday

23. The spirituality of a cathedral—the nave
Preached at Evensong on the First Sunday in Lent 2019

24. The spirituality of a cathedral—the choir
Preached at Evensong on the Second Sunday in Lent 2019

25. The spirituality of a cathedral—the altar
Preached at Evensong on the Third Sunday in Lent 2019

26. The spirituality of a cathedral—the flags
Preached at Evensong on the Fourth Sunday in Lent 2019

27. Held in the story of God
Preached on Christmas Day 2019

28. Simeon's song
Luke 2:22–40

Preached at Evensong on 31 January 2021 for the Feast of the Presentation of Christ in the Temple

29. Layers removed
Psalm 25:1–10; Mark 1:9–15
Preached on the First Sunday in Lent 2021

30. We wish to see Jesus
Preached on Good Friday 2022

31. Startled by Jesus
Ezekiel 37:1–14; Psalm 115; Luke 24:1–12
Preached on 11 April 2021

32. Tears pouring down his cheeks
Matthew 22:15–33
Preached on 22 October 2023

33. Allowing God to be God
Isaiah 55:1–9; Luke 13:1–9
Preached on 20 March 2022

34. Standing under a waterfall
John 3:14–21
Preached on 14 March 2021

35. Known by name
John 10:22–30
Preached on 8 May 2022

36. Thriving in God
John 15:1–8
Preached on 2 May 2021

37. Sitting in a ditch
Amos 7:7–17; Luke 10:25–37

Preached on 14 July 2019

38. All are welcome
Jeremiah 2:4–13; Luke 14:1–14
Preached on 28 August 2022